Stress Less 2 Coloring Book

30 Intricate detail full page mandalas for coloring in

for relaxation and stress relief

By Artist

Dwyanna Stoltzfus

Join the Fun!!

Share your colored pages!!

You are invited to color the pages
From this and all publications by
Dwyanna Stoltzfus. Then scan and post
Your colored creations in
Coloring with Dwyanna
Adult Coloring Group
On facebook
https://web.facebook.com/groups/1519357628356169/?_rdr
Join Coloring with Dwyanna Coloring Group,
And have fun sharing your colored pages
And meeting new coloring friends.
Members of the group will also have access
To free coloring pages.
You are welcome to share your colored pages on
Any social network, make sure to mention the title of
The book and the author/artist name.
Uncolored images may not be shared.

About:

Get ready to color 30 fantastic stress relieving patterns by Artist Dwyanna Stoltzfus.
In this adult coloring book you will find 30 beautiful illustrations, printed one per page.
A collection of wonderful detailed mandala patterns that relax you and melt away stress
and tension as you color. You can use this coloring book to help you relax and
unwind after a long day. Or you can use it just for fun.
You can color the designs simply or add depth and creativity by
shading and highlighting. Crayons are not recommended for
the intricate designs. You can color with fine tip markers, gel pens,
colored pencils and fine liners. Enjoy the experience of coloring!!
But most of all relax and have fun!!

Coloring tips:

If you desire to add depth to your coloring you can shade with colored pencils.
Use dark colors around edges and into the peaks. Blend in light colors for the
middle and more open spaces. You can use black to darken areas,
and white to lighten and brighten areas.

Acknowledgments

Thank You to my family for all your support
of my art and this project.
I could not have done it without you!!

Thank You God for the gift and love
Of art and drawing!!

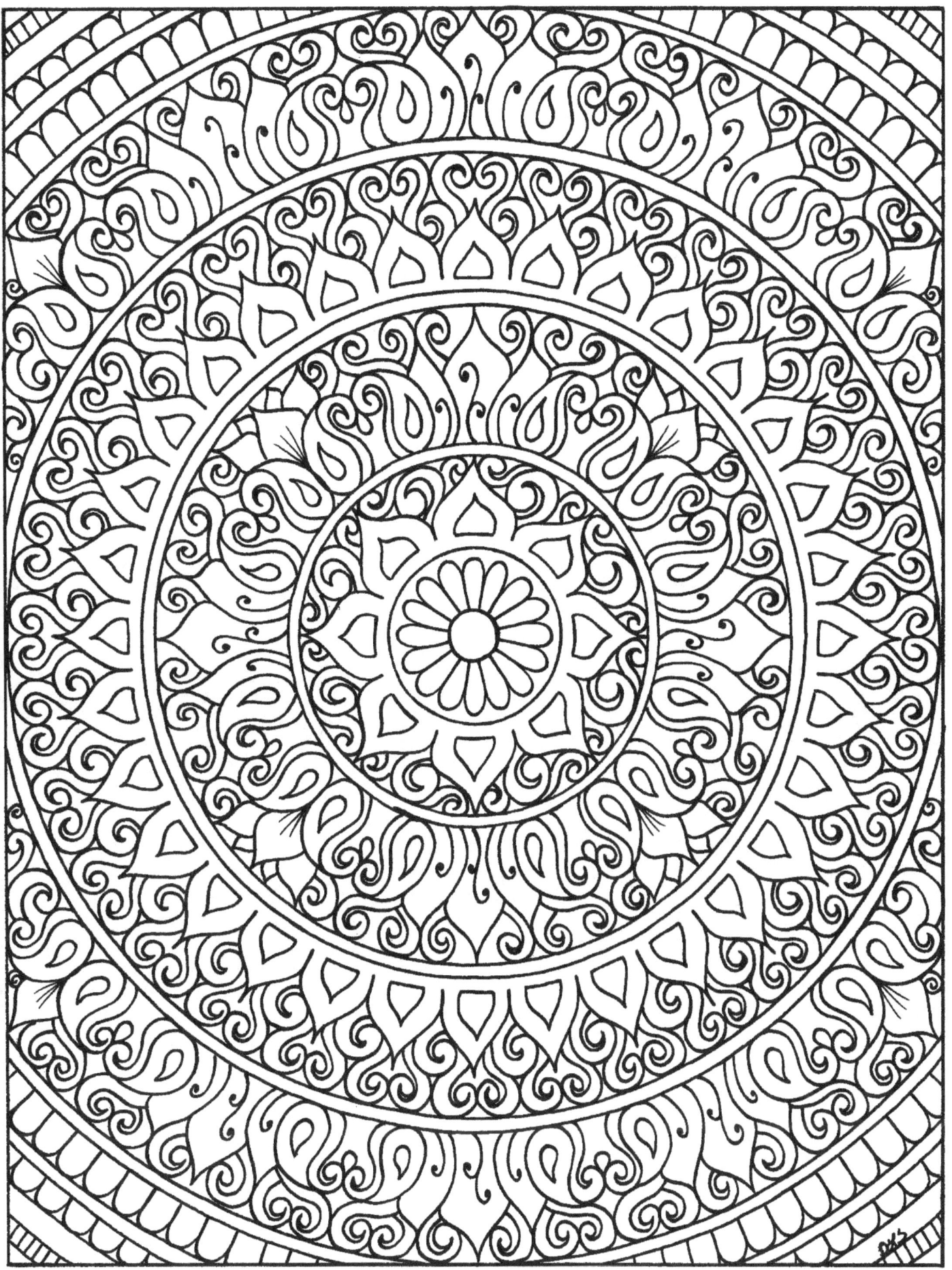

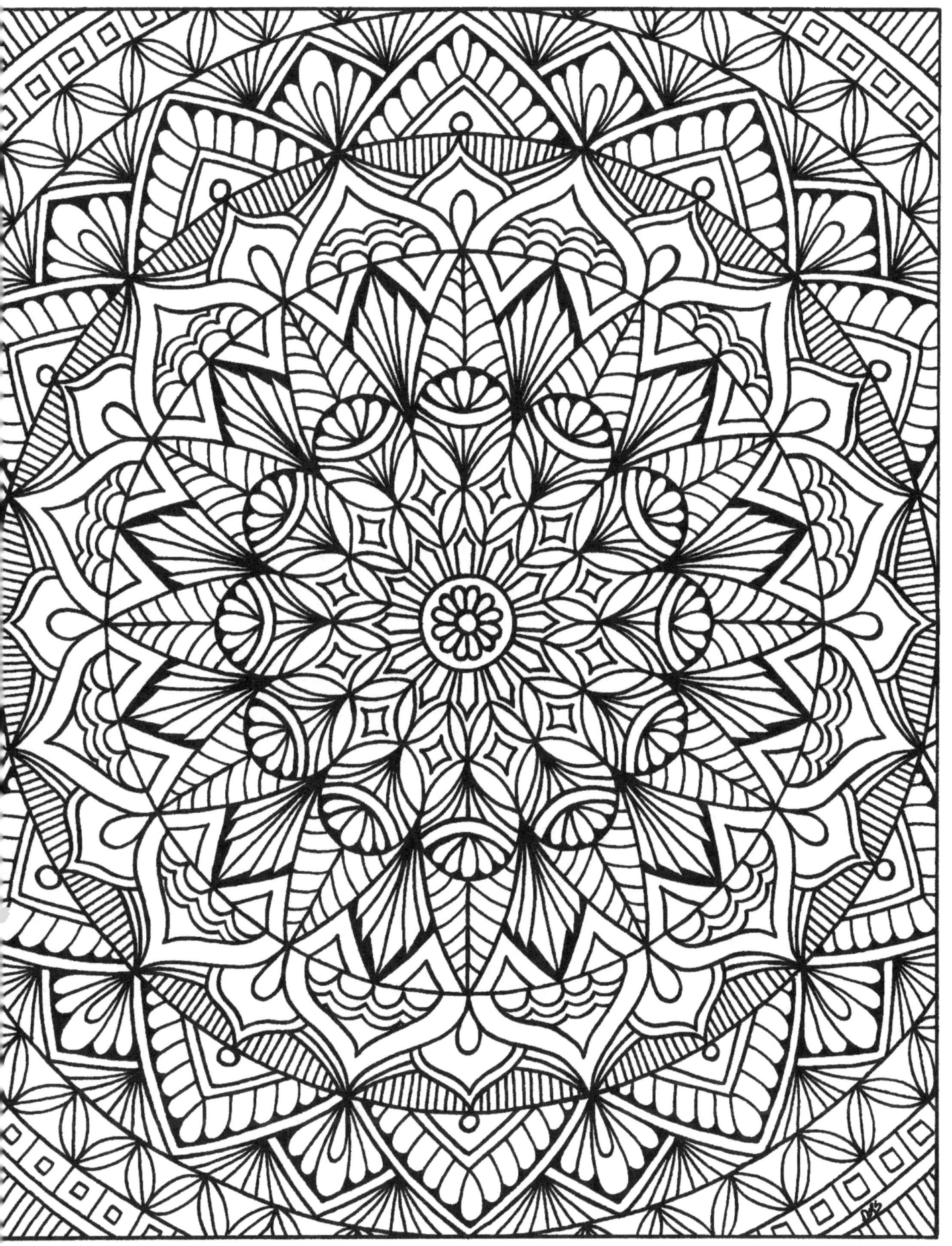

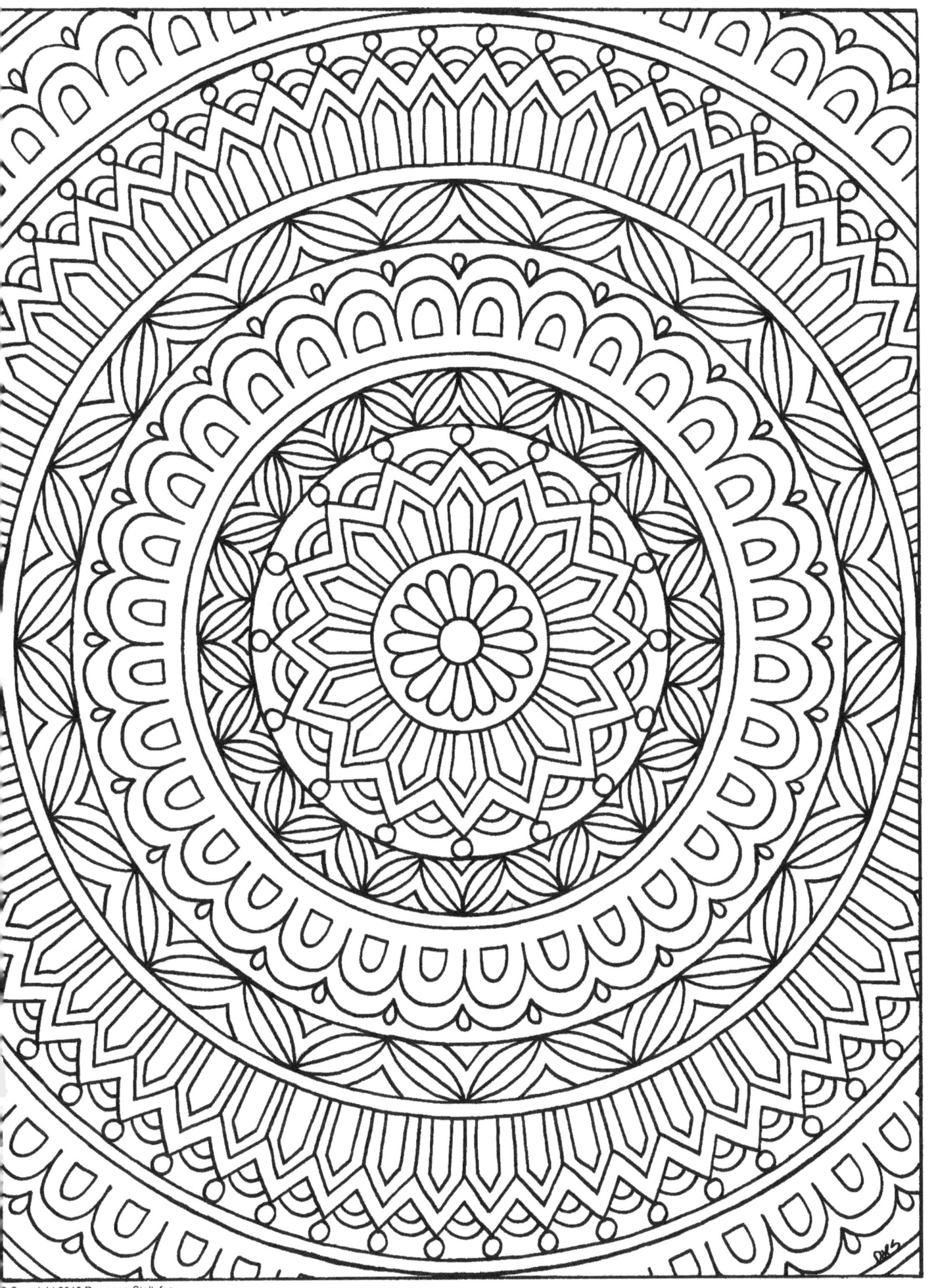

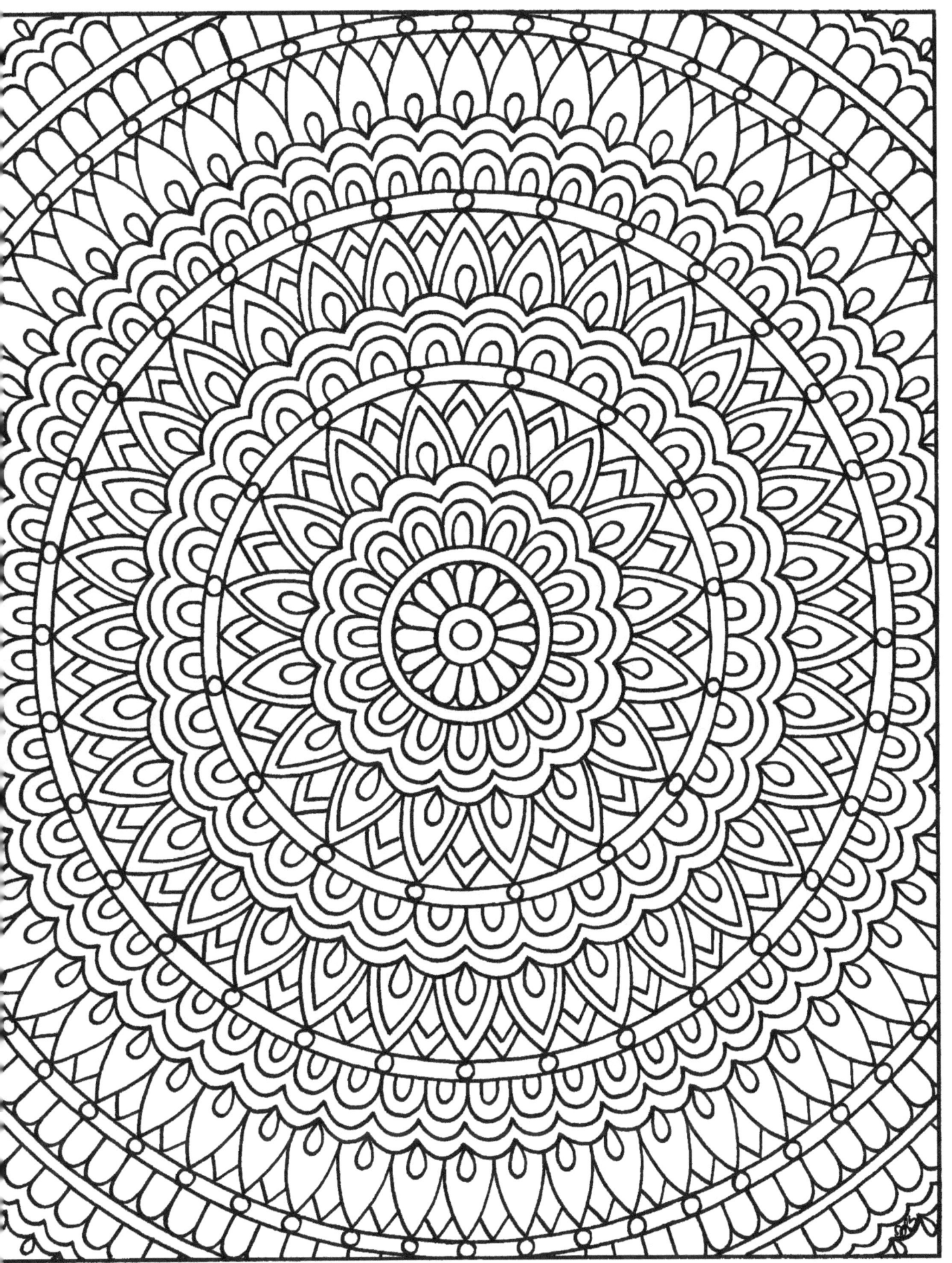

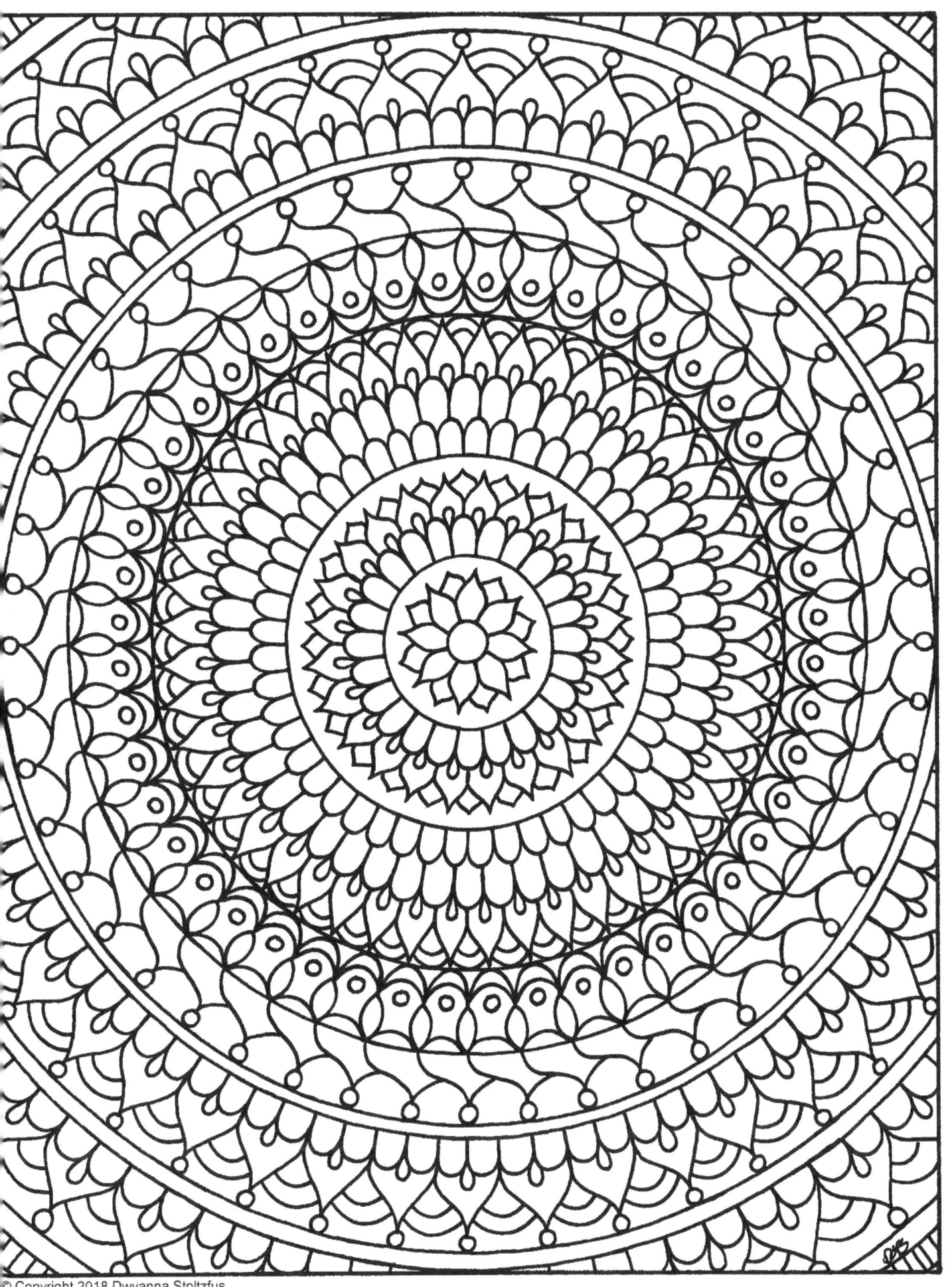

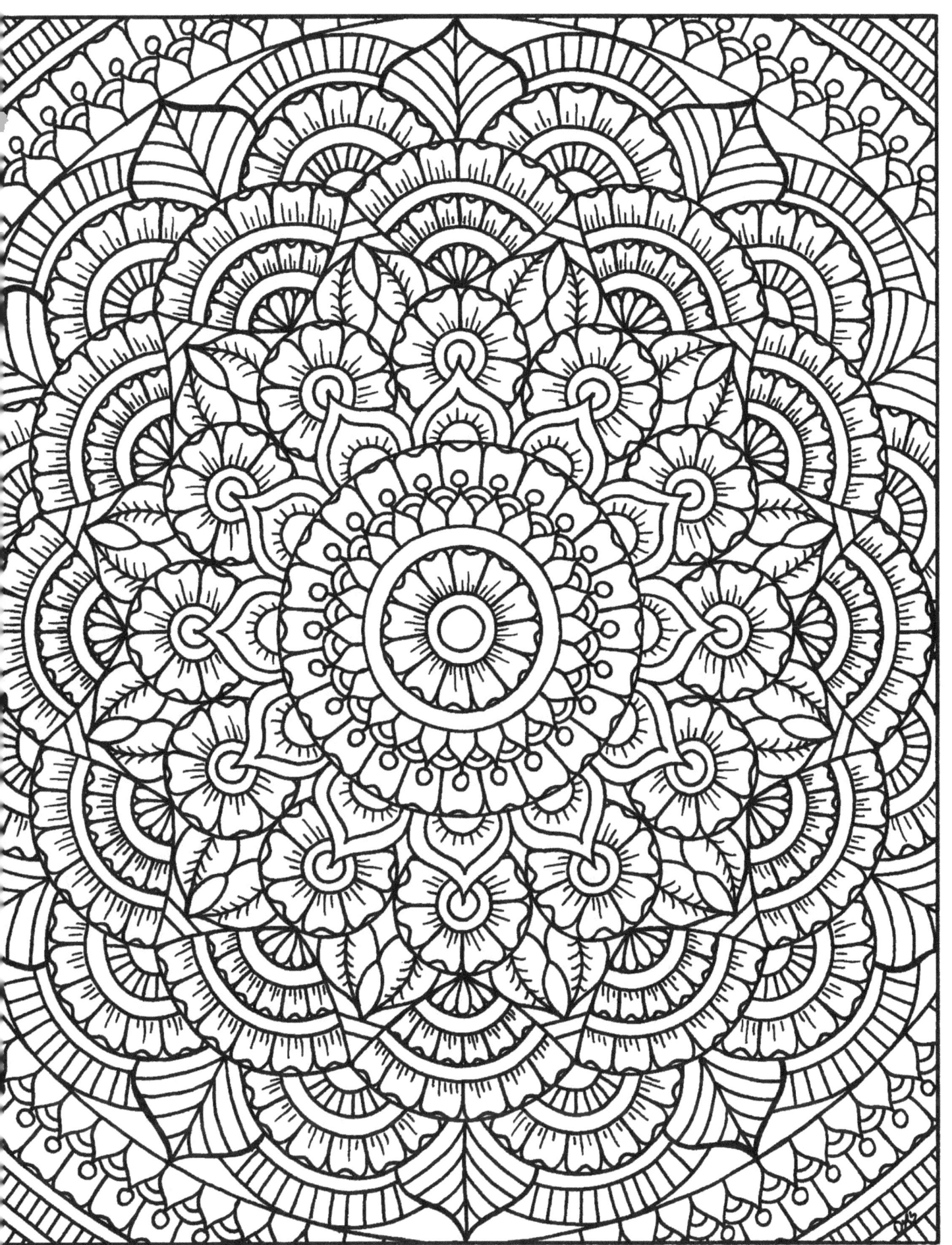

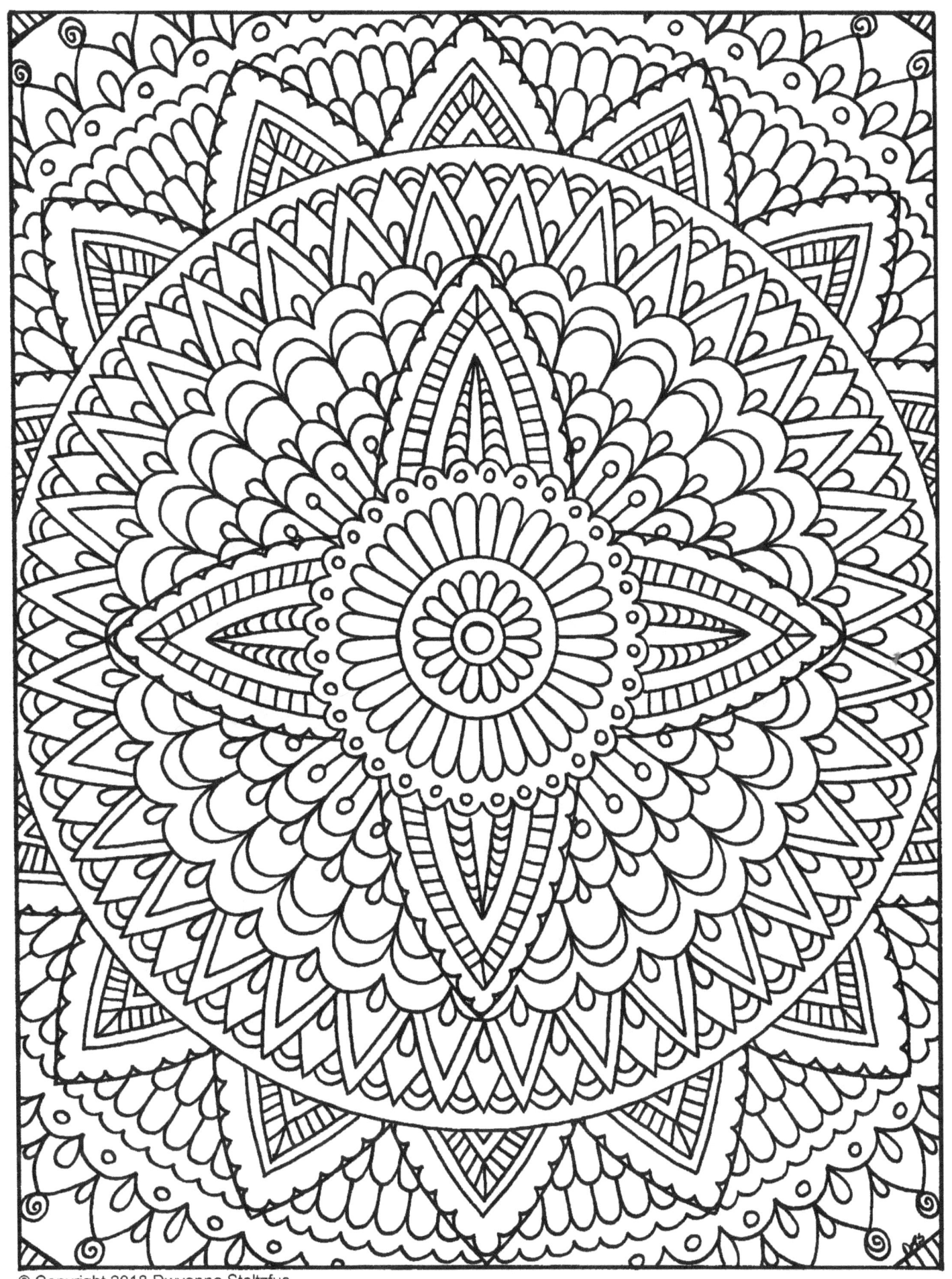

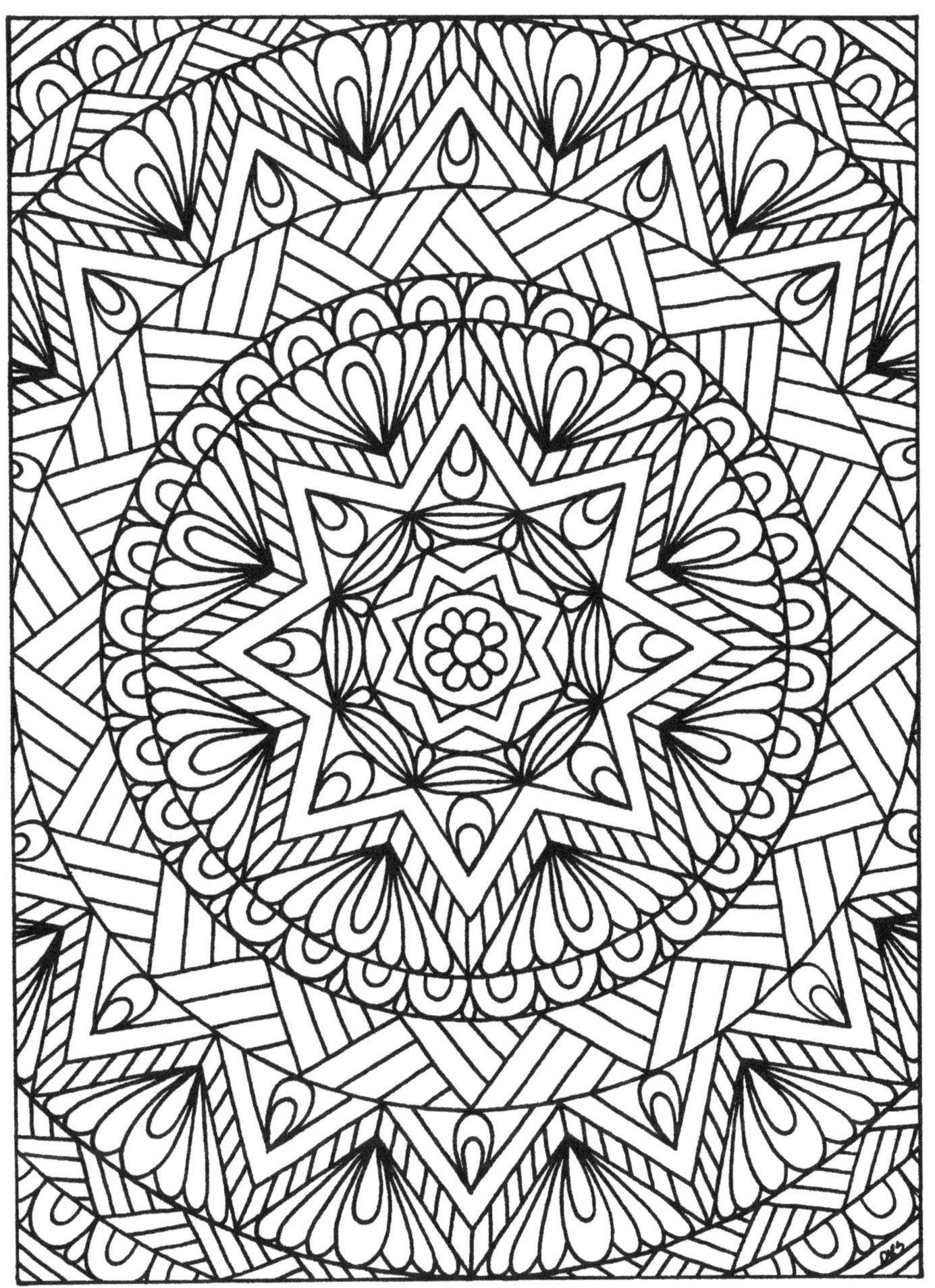

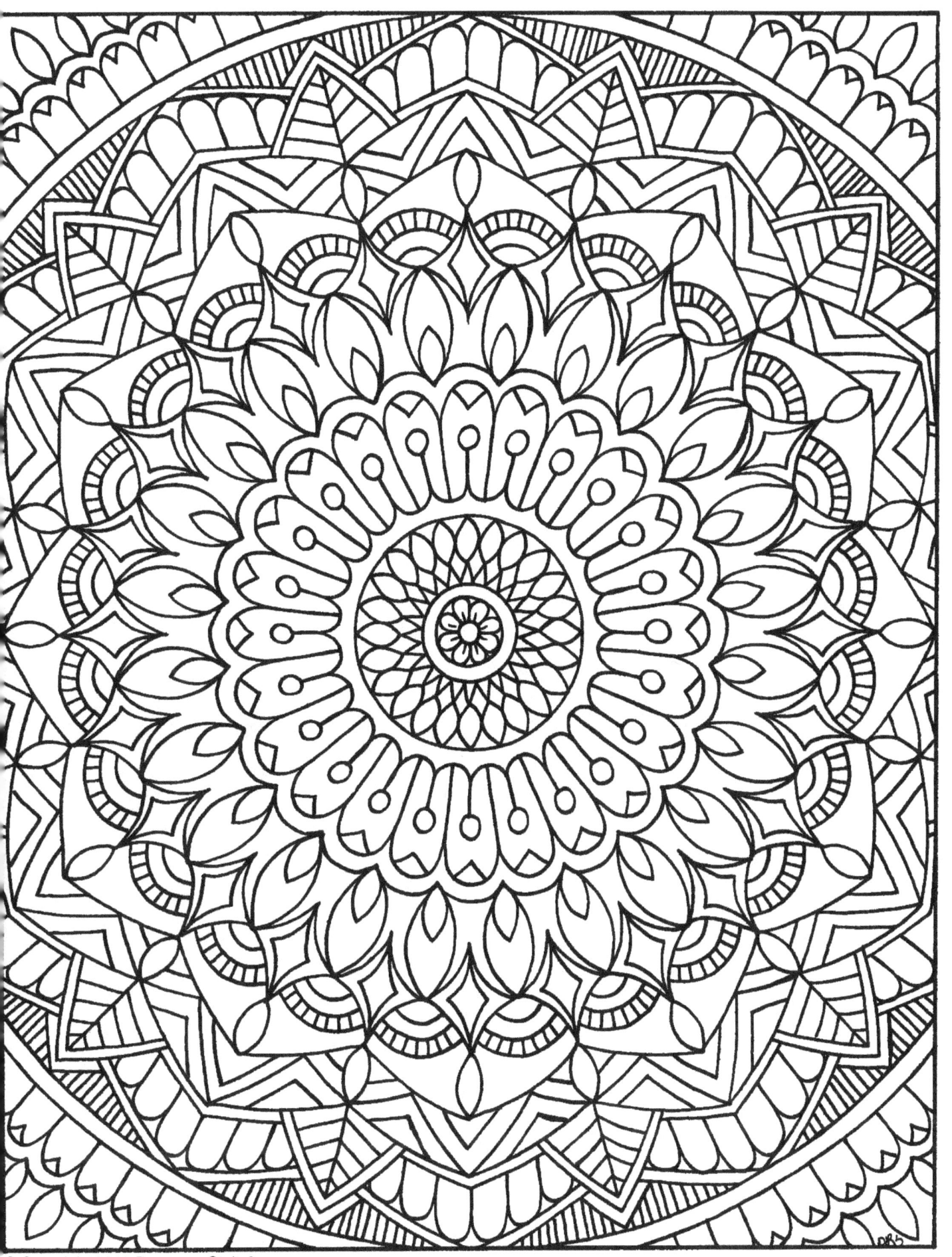

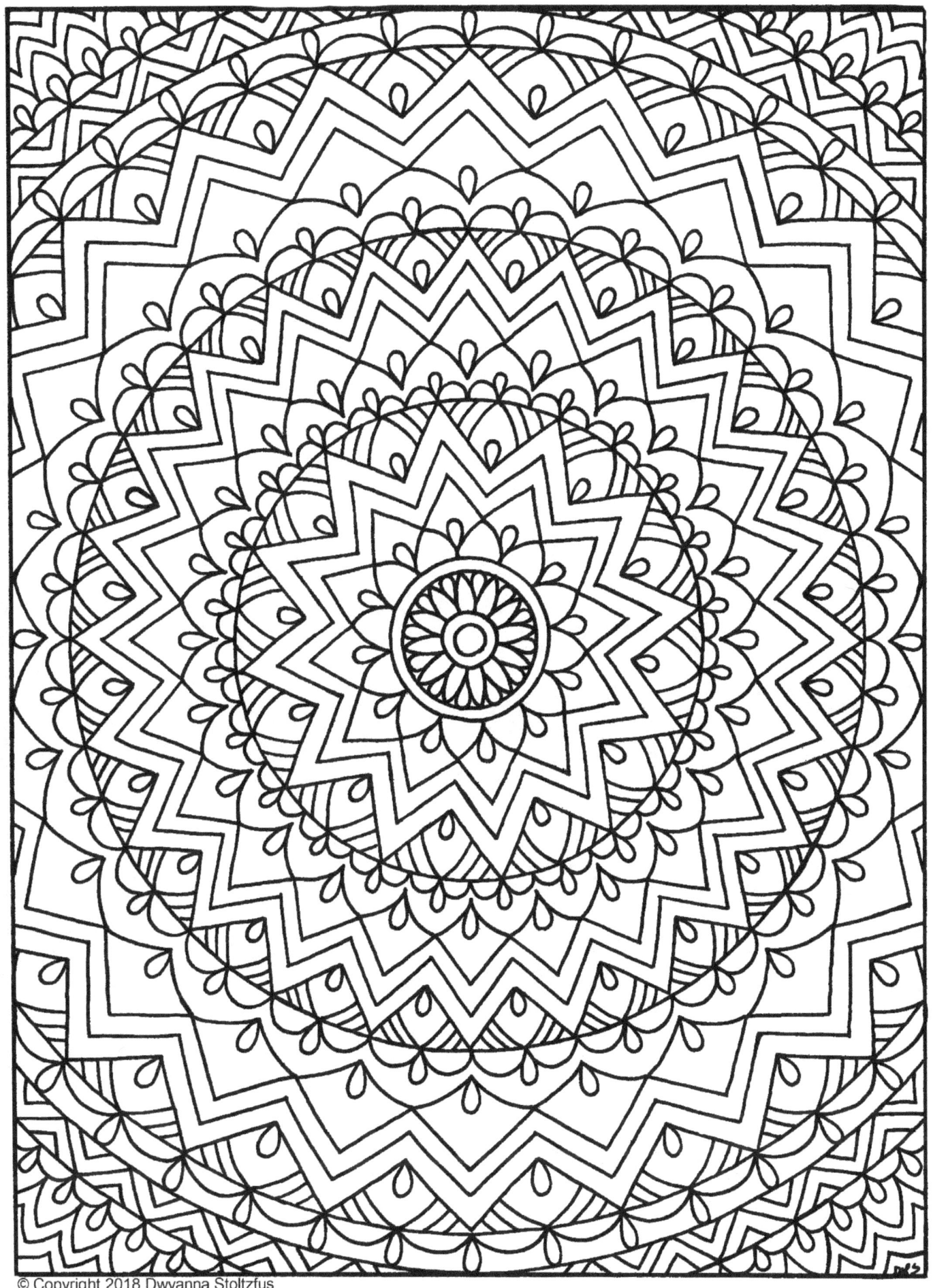

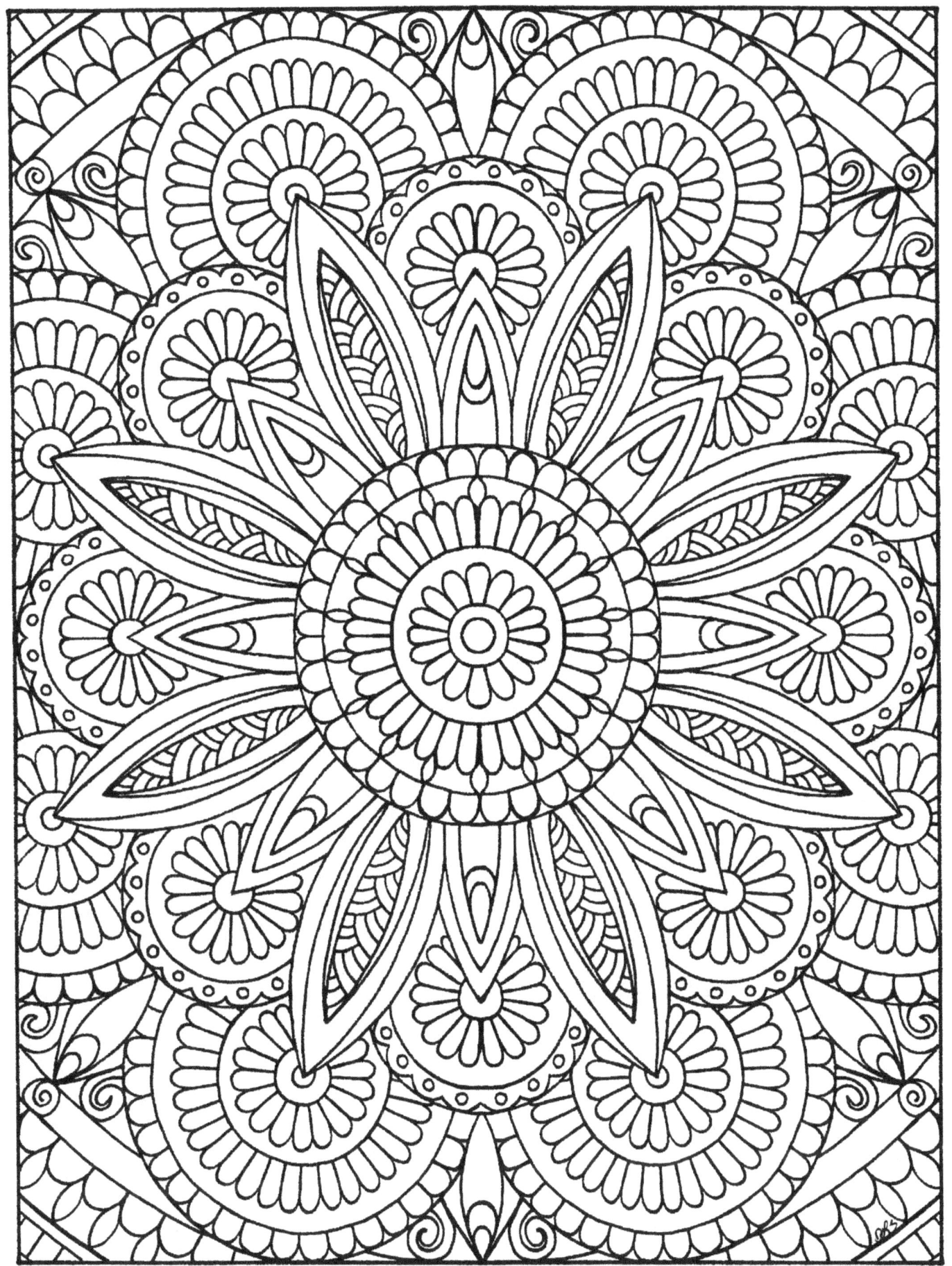

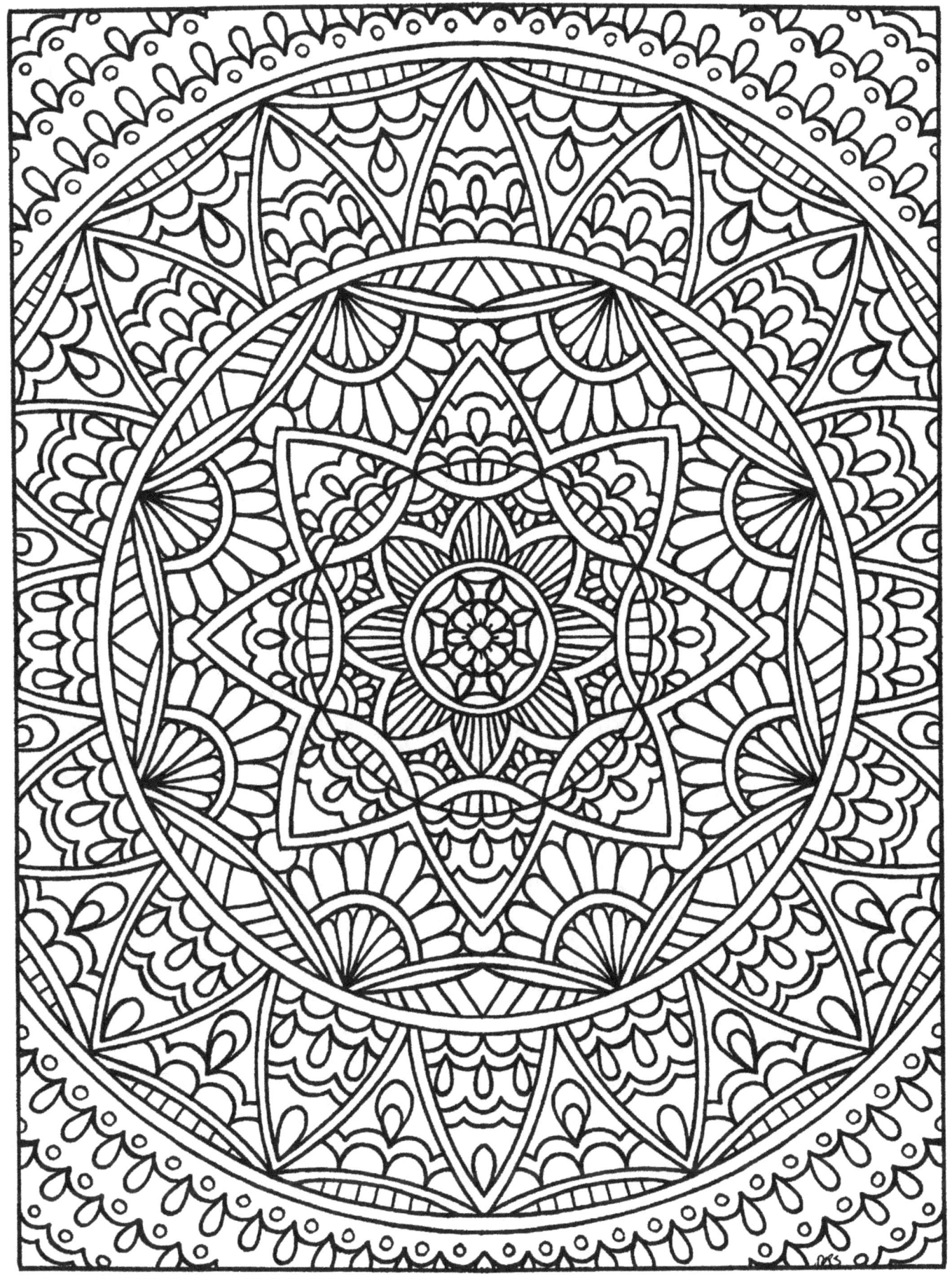

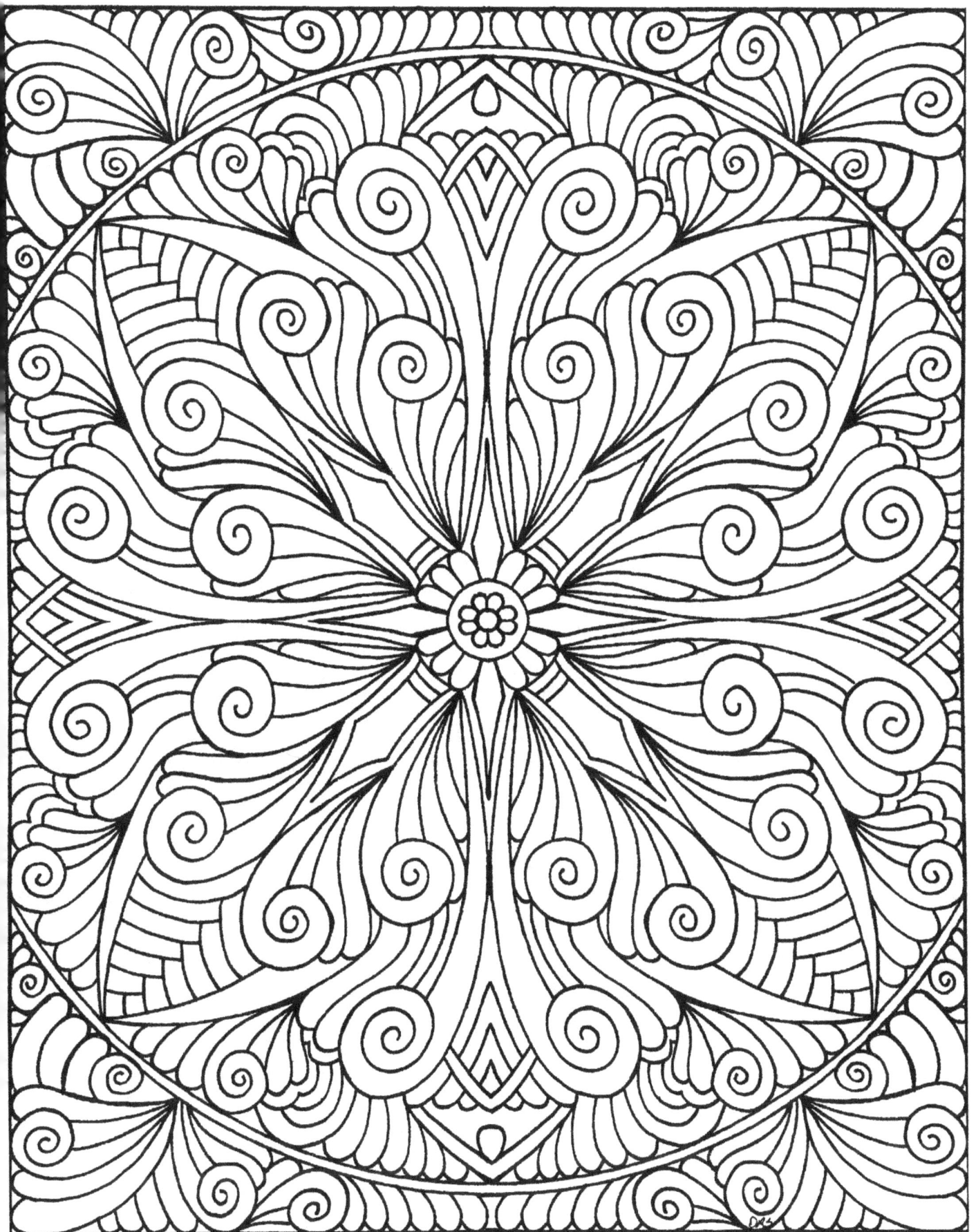

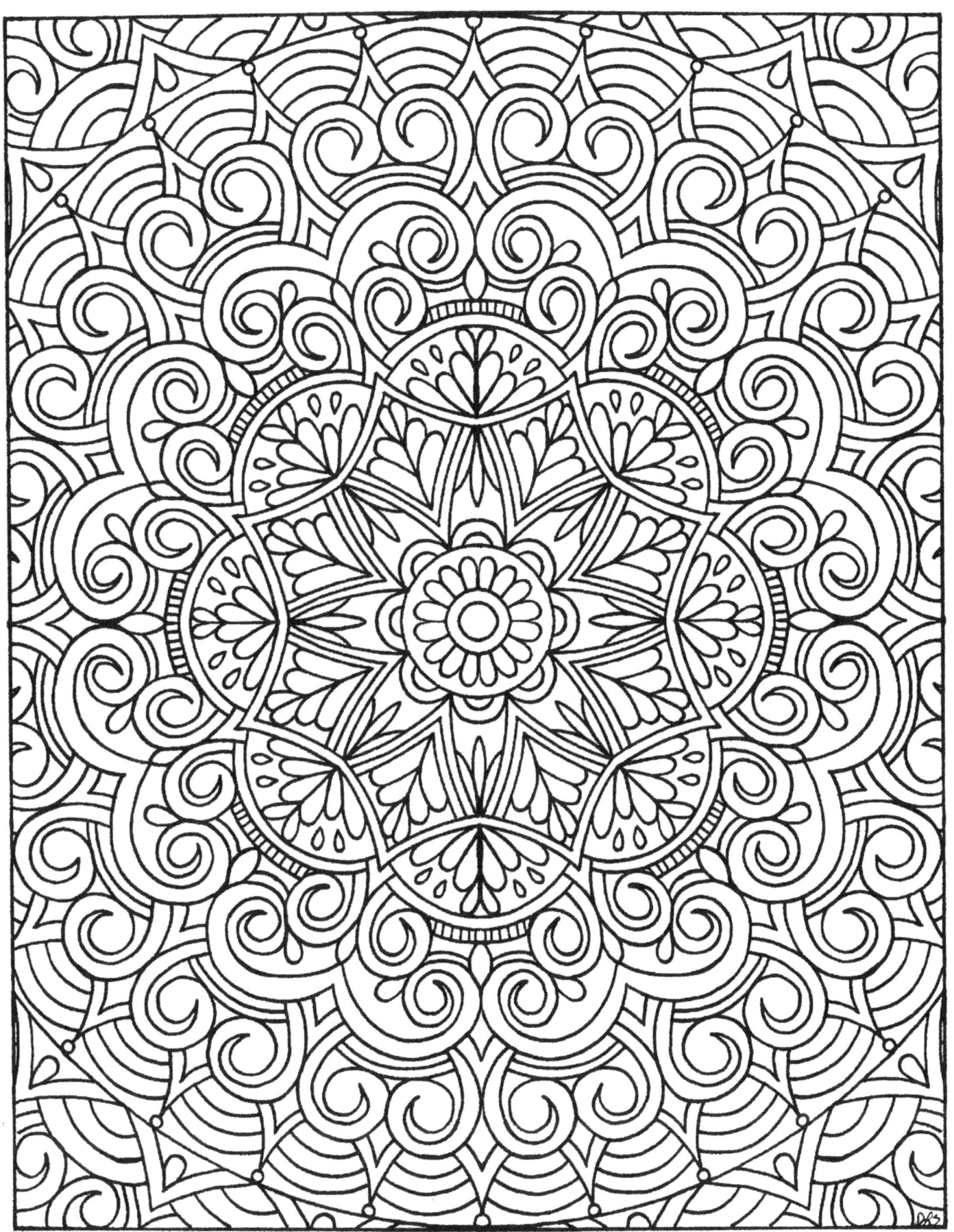

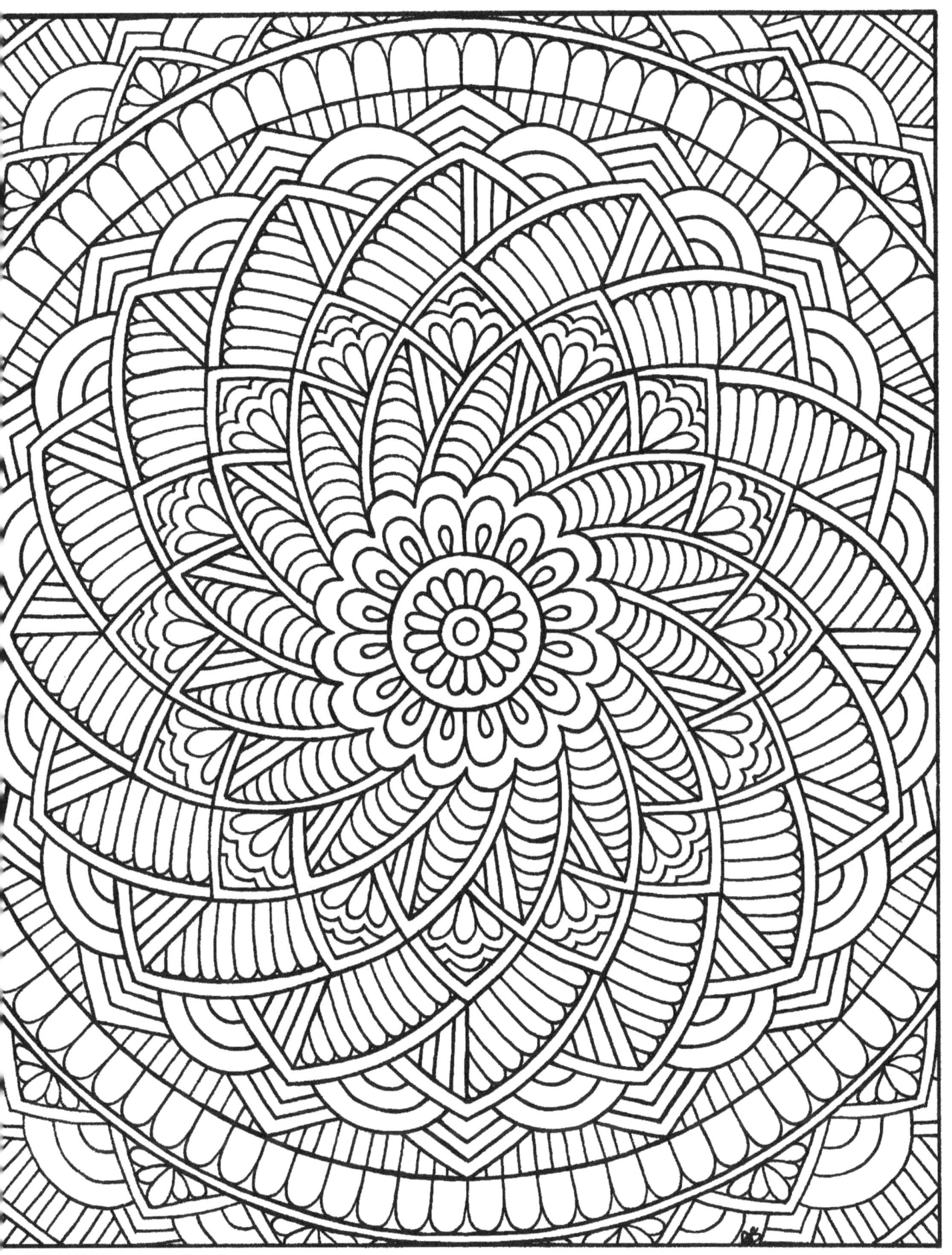

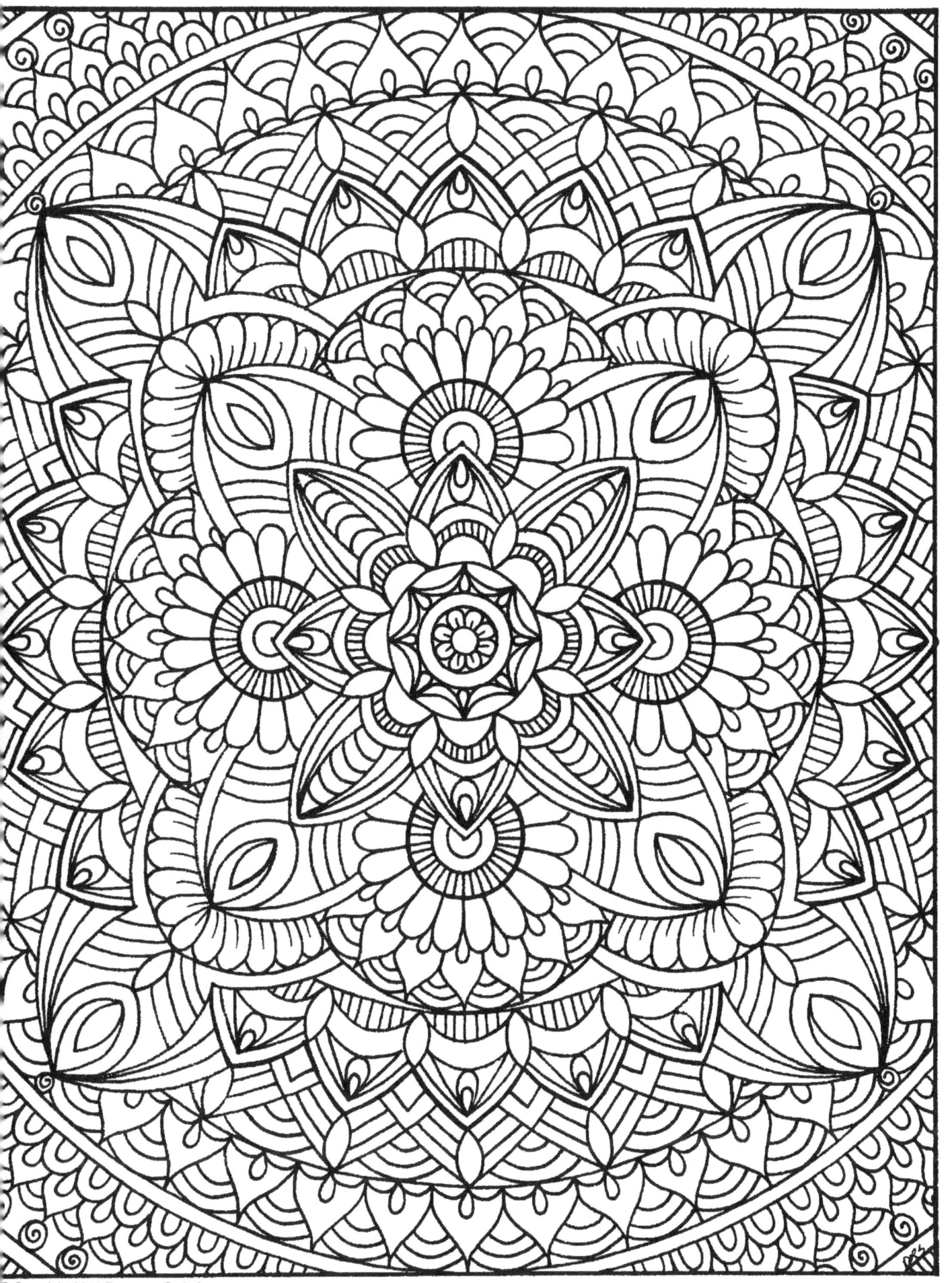

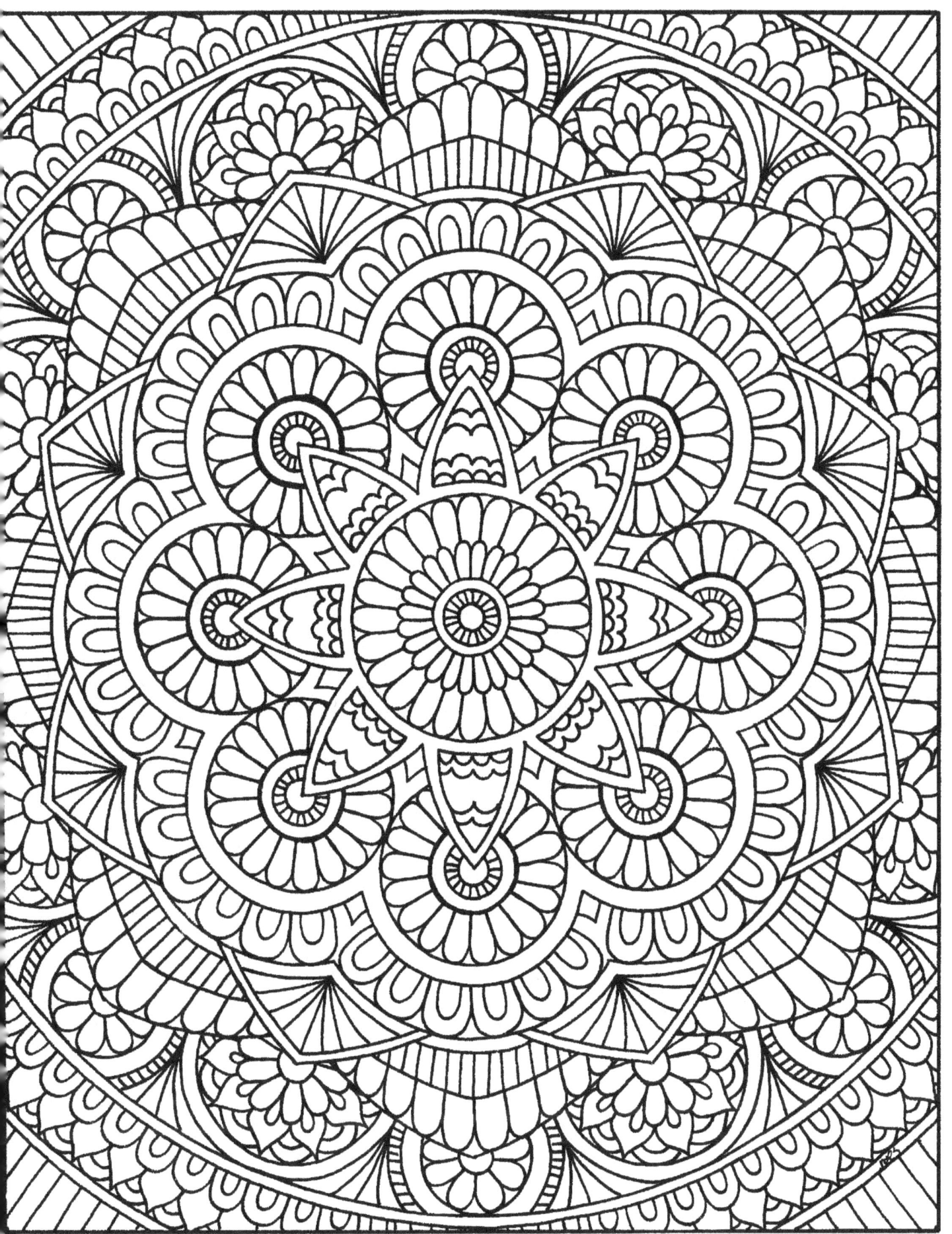

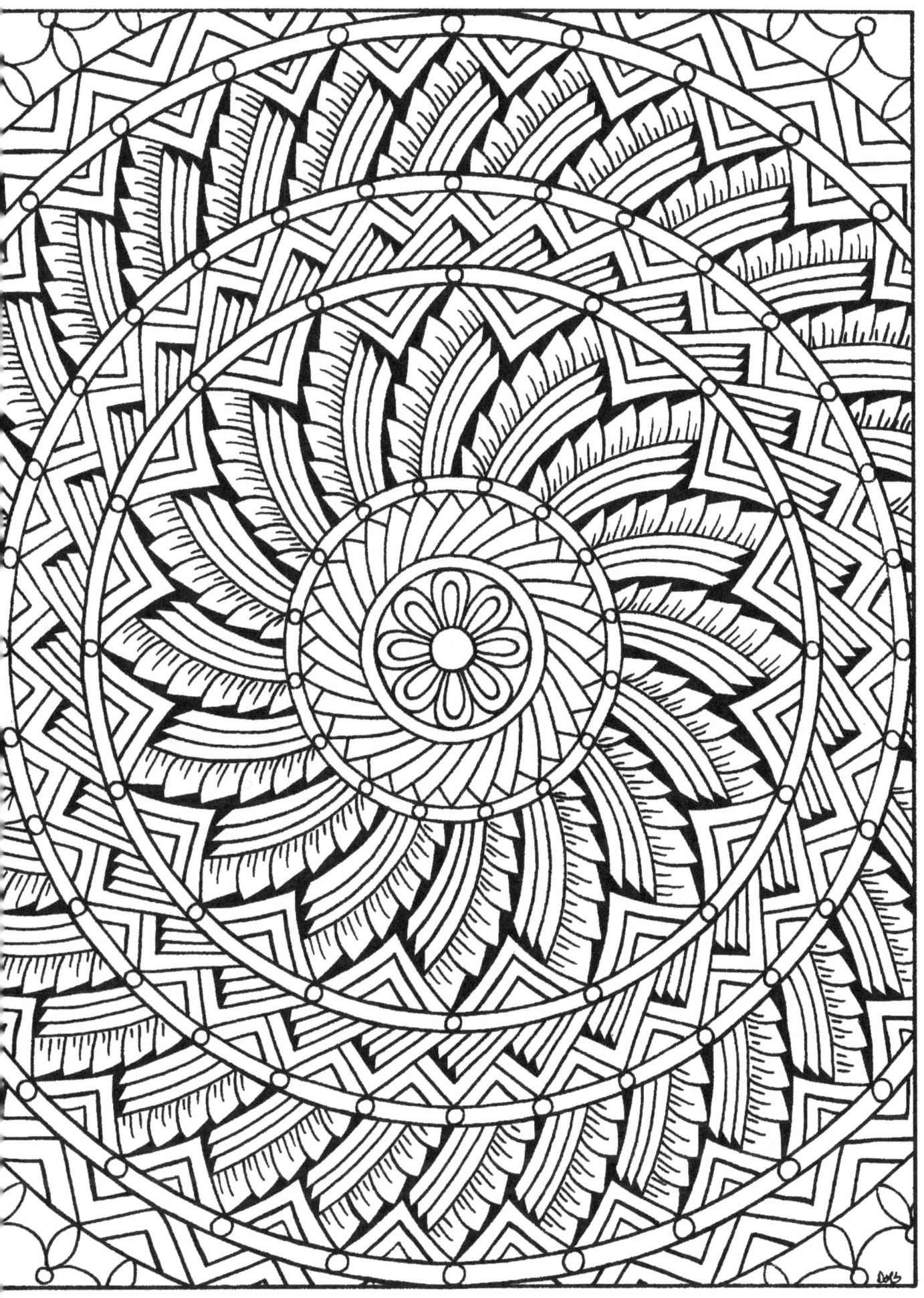

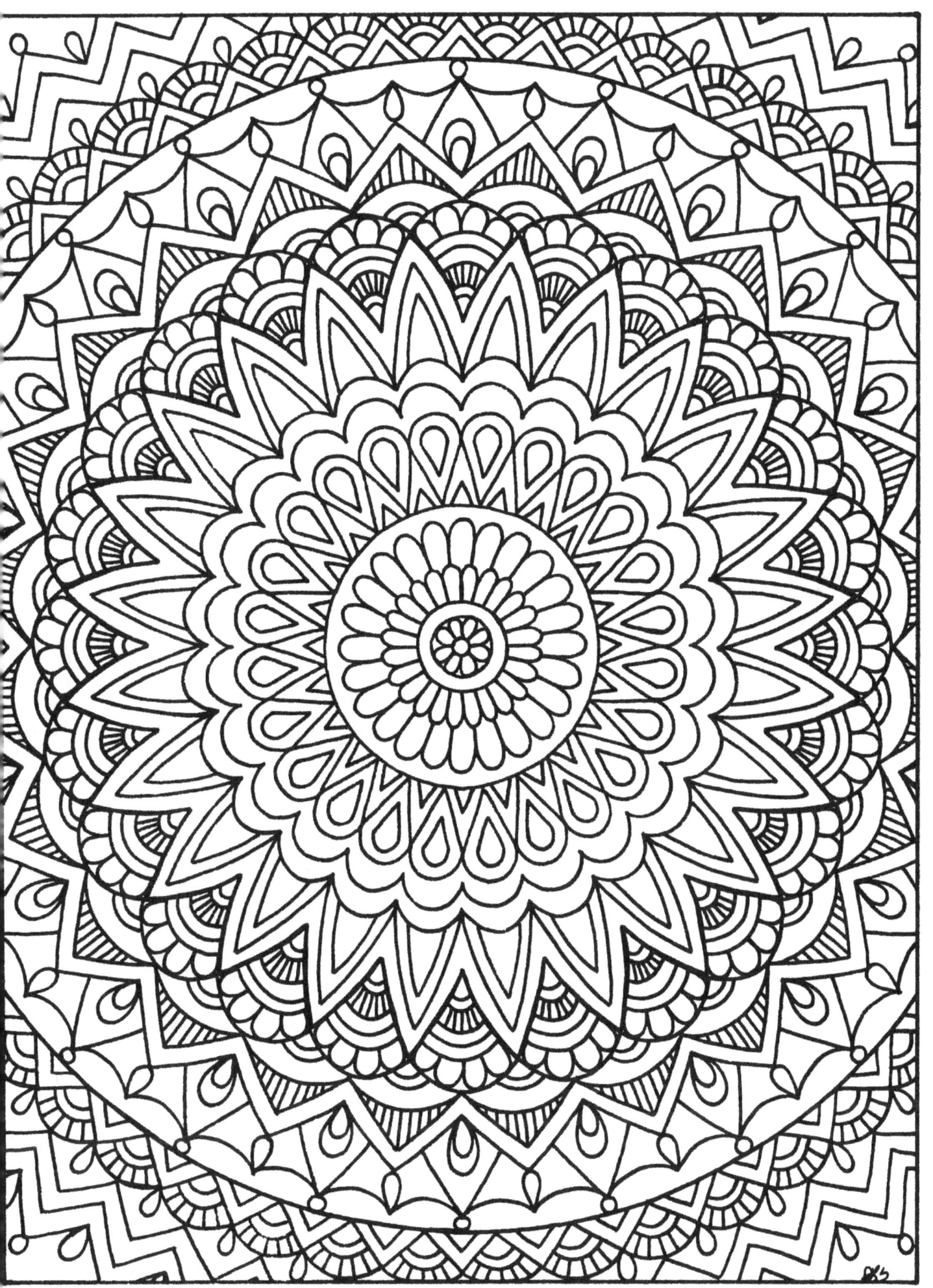

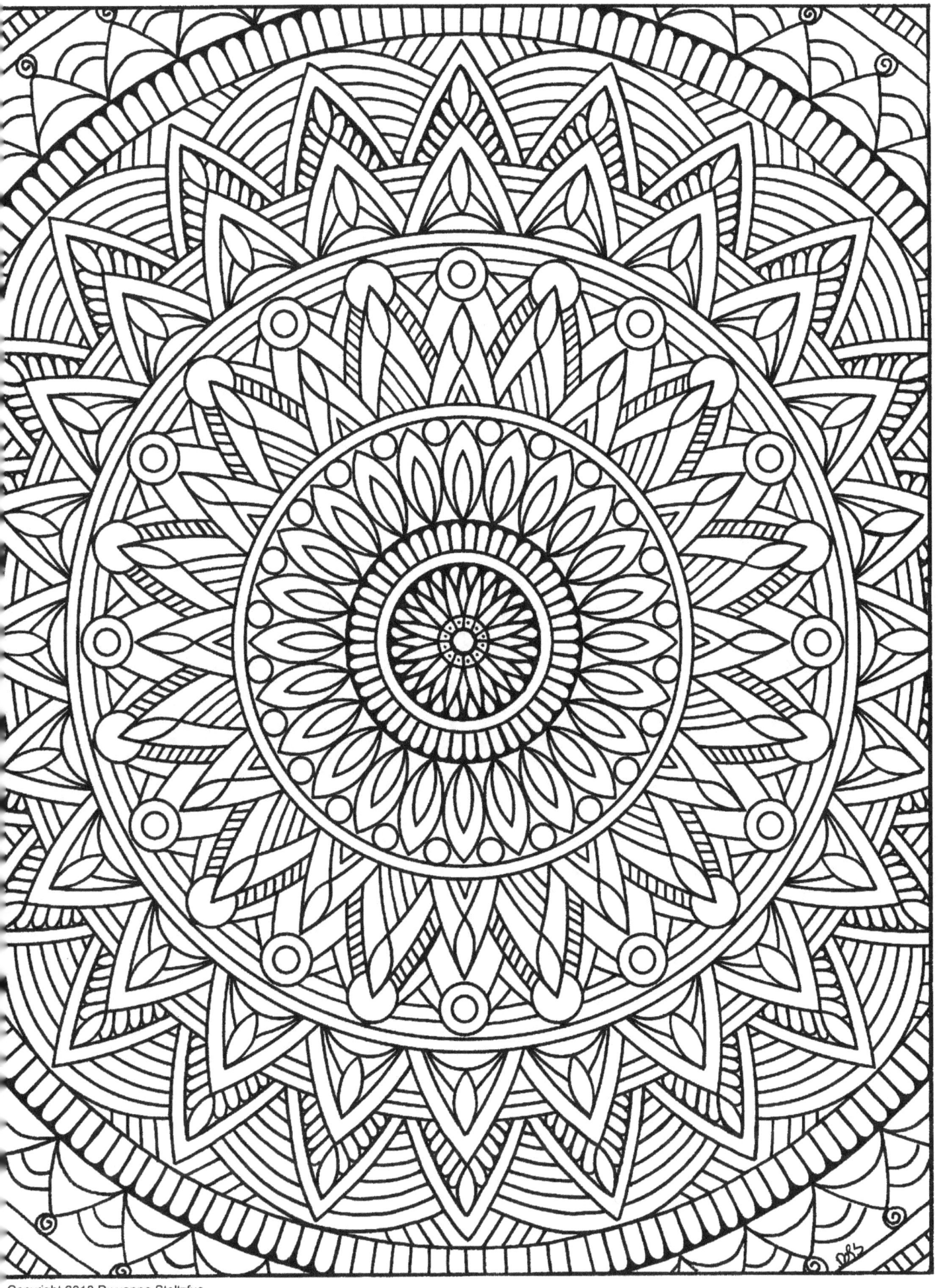

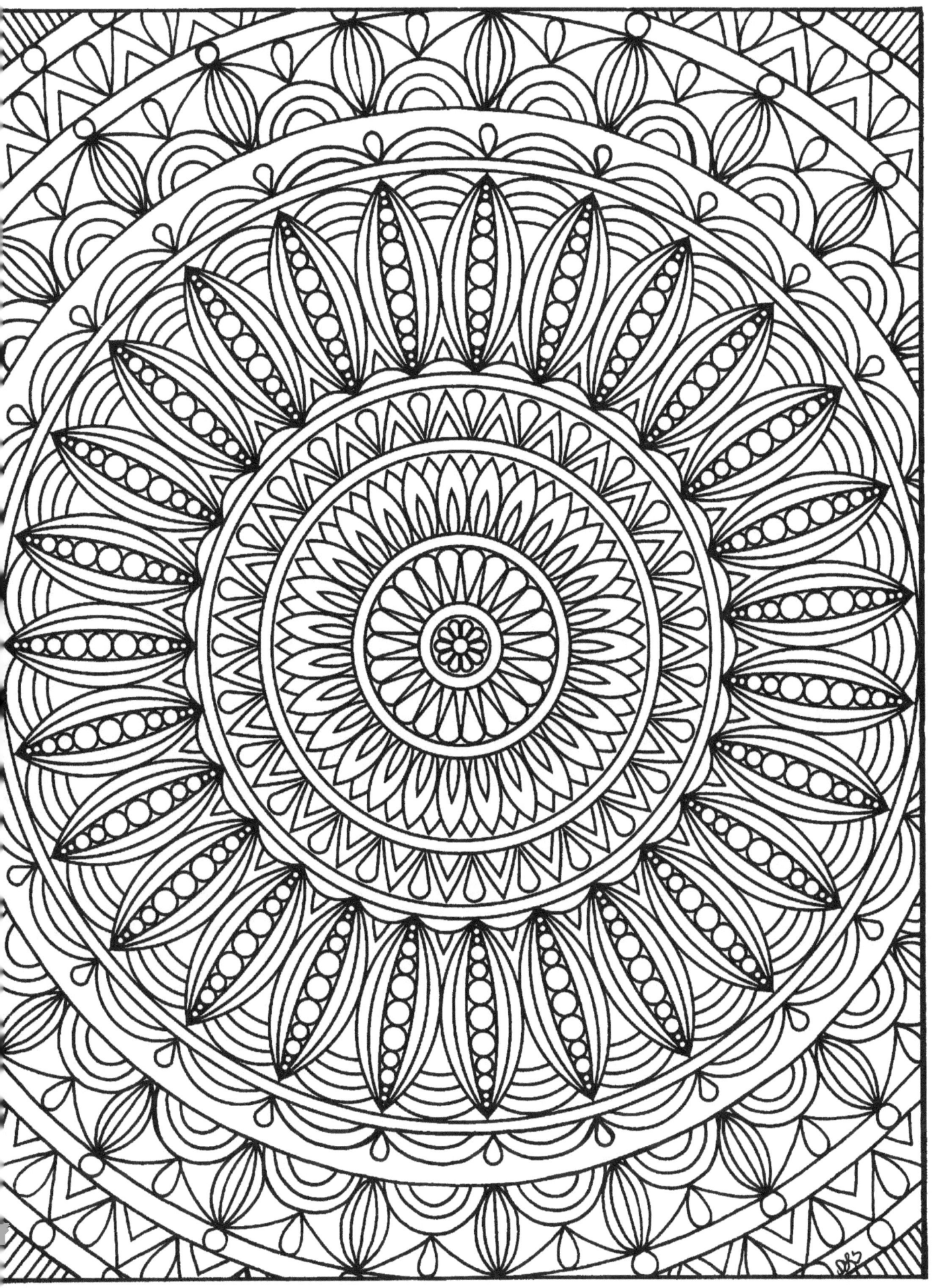

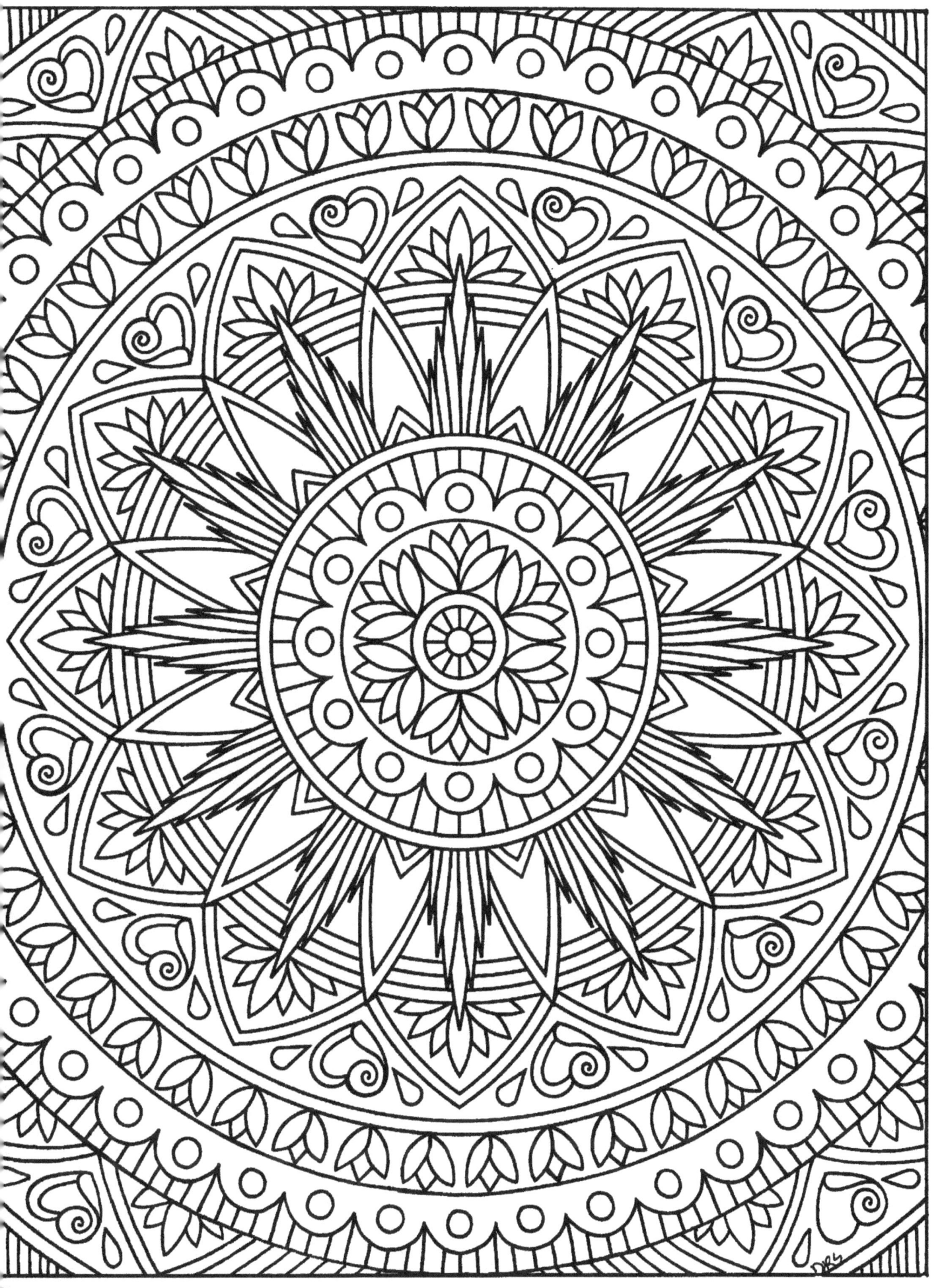

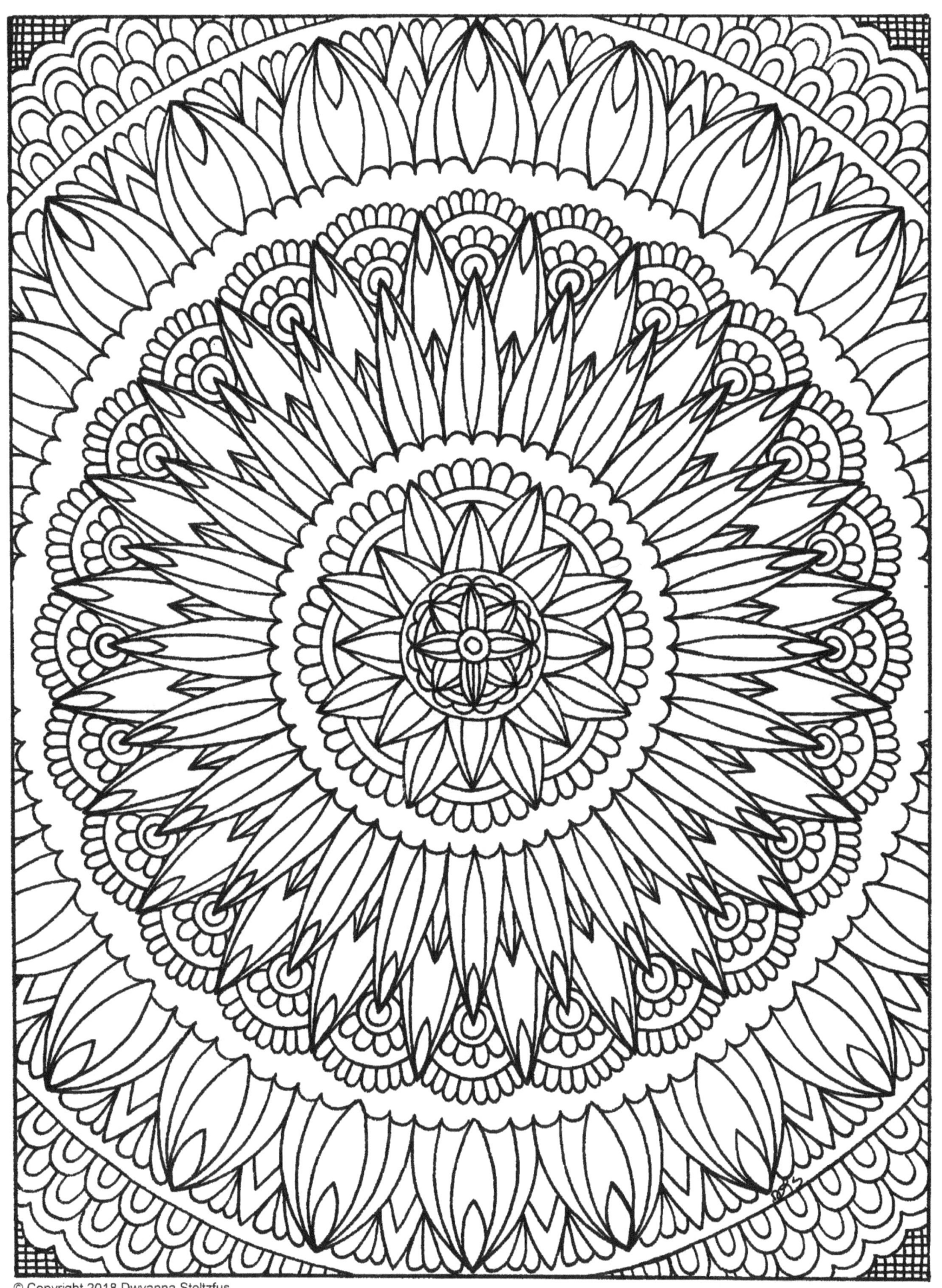

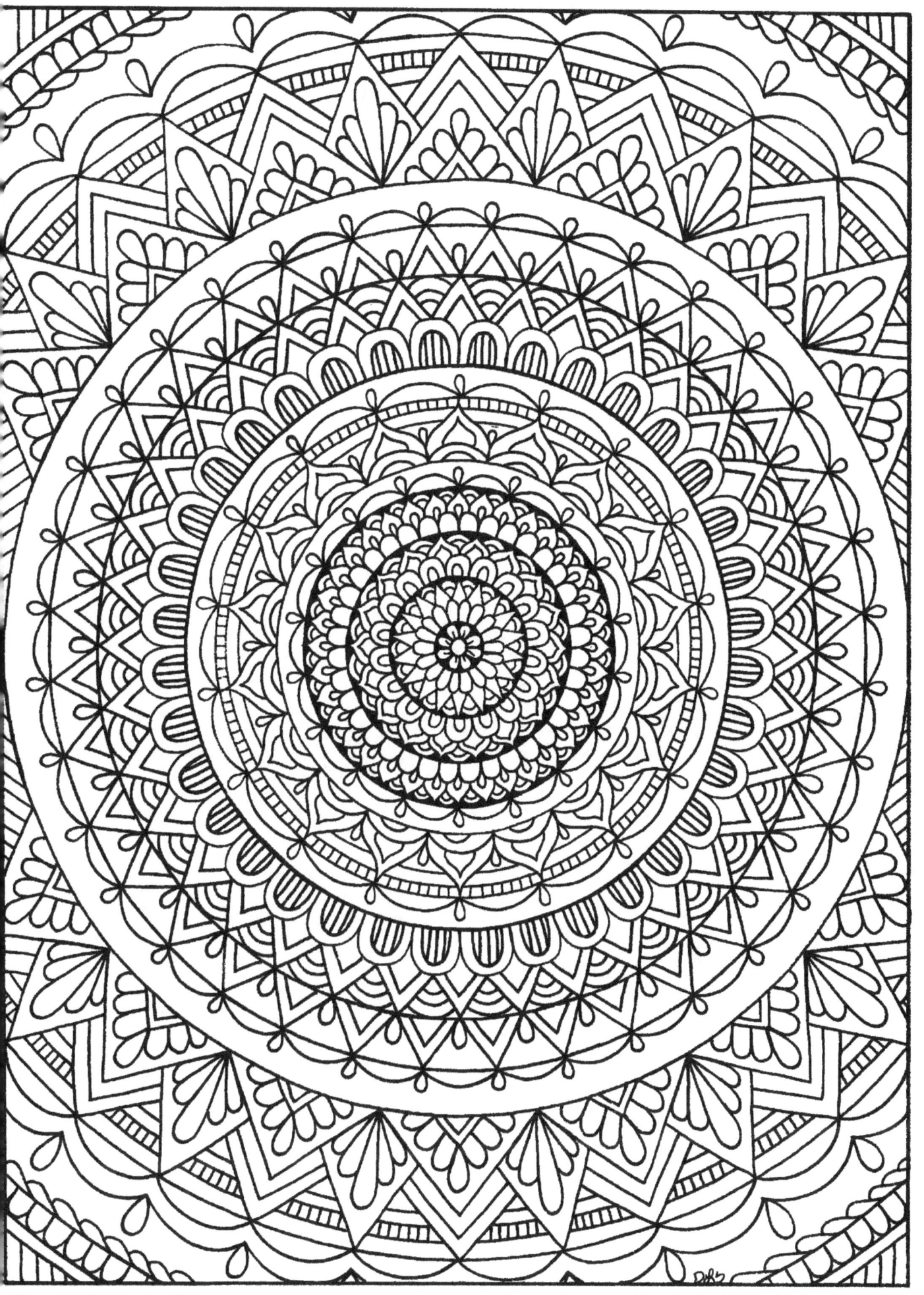

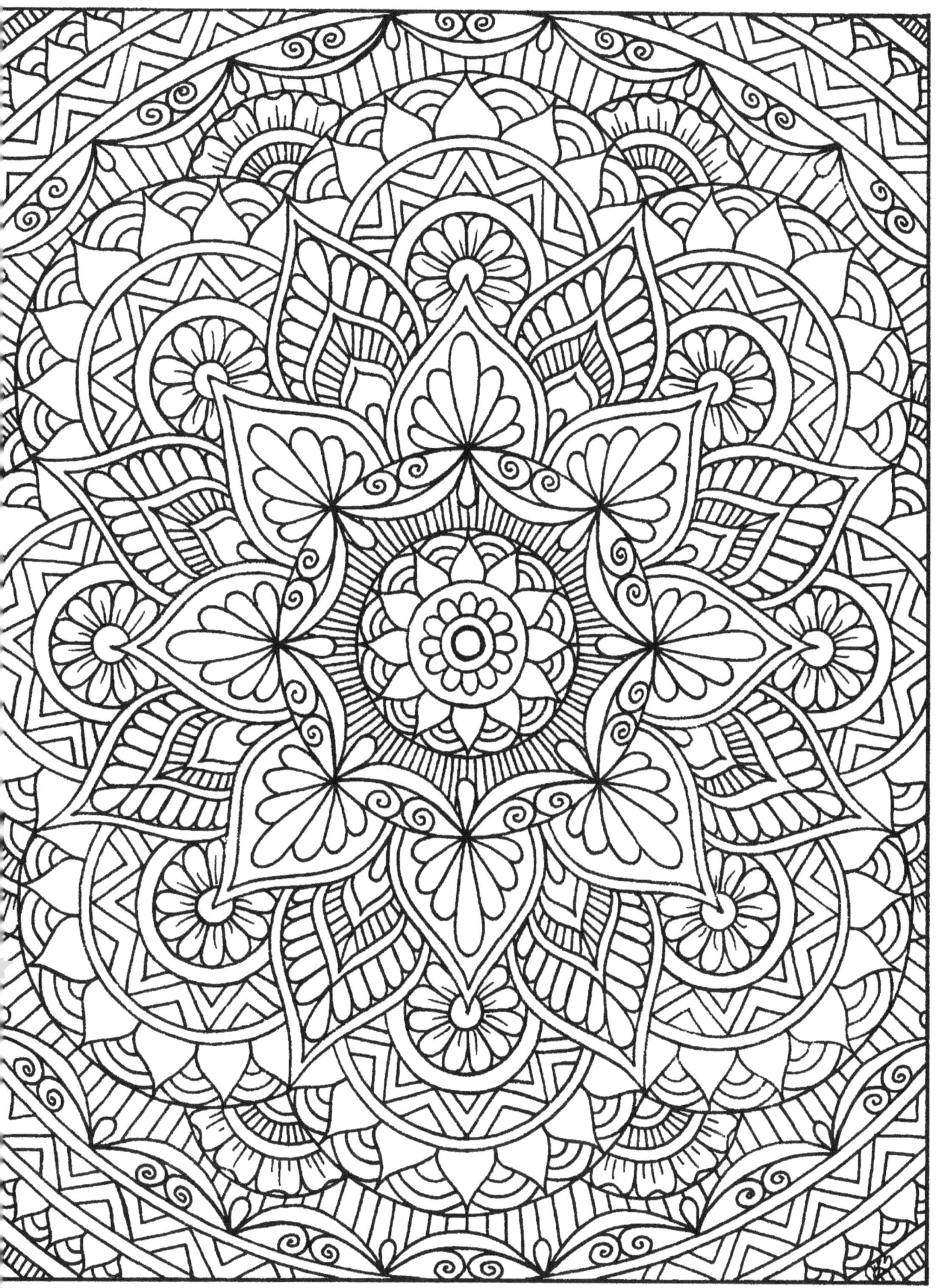

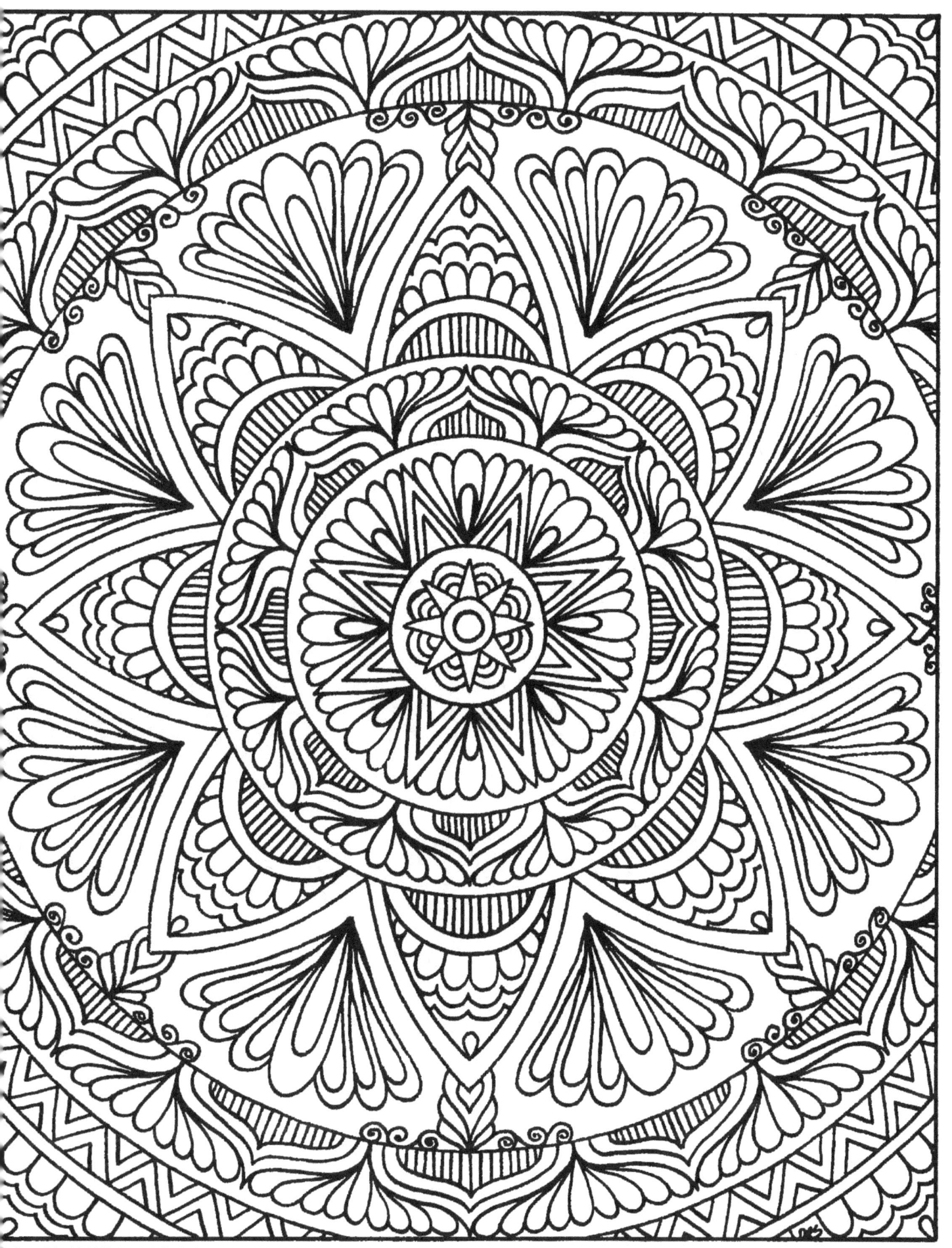

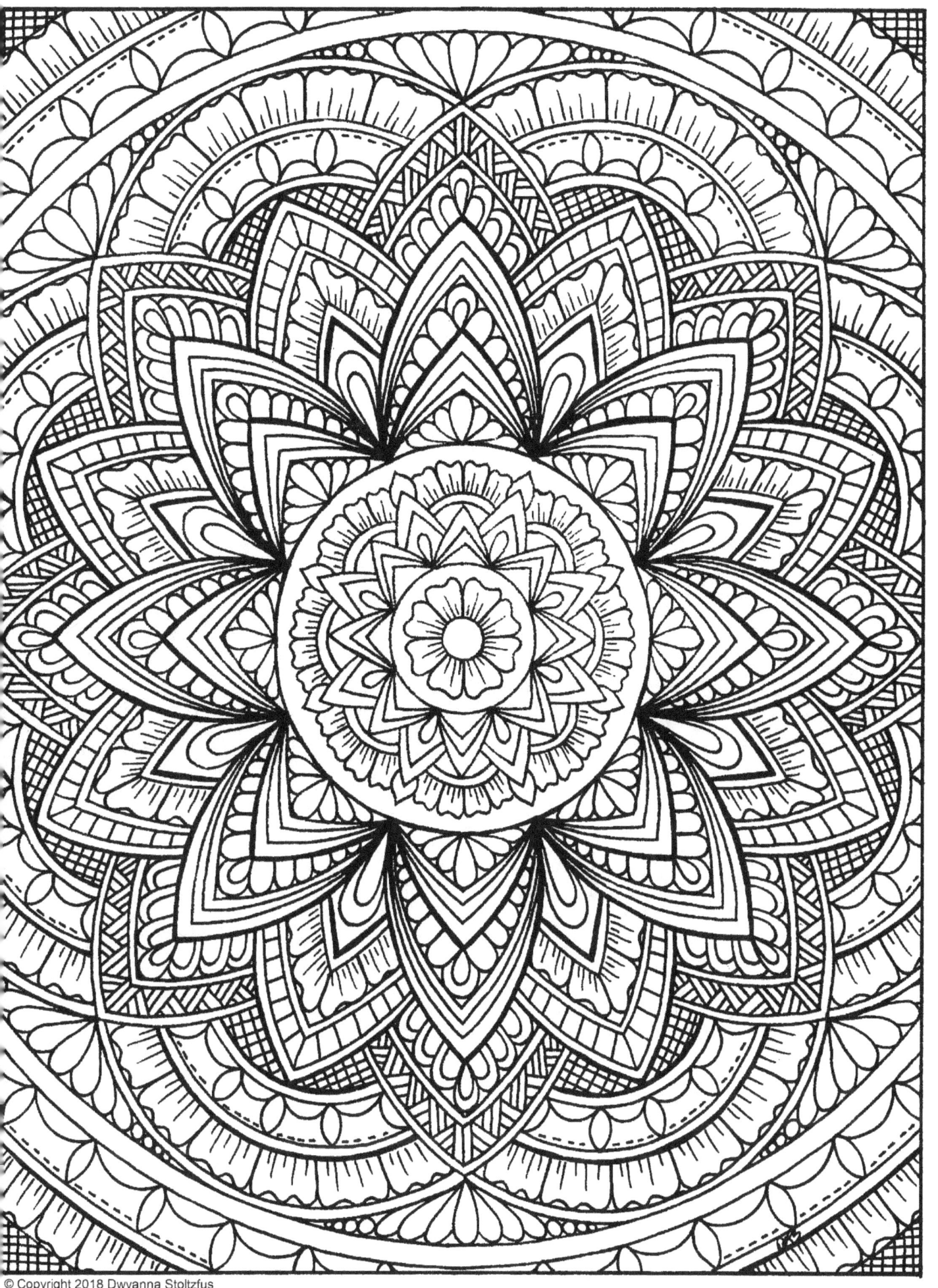

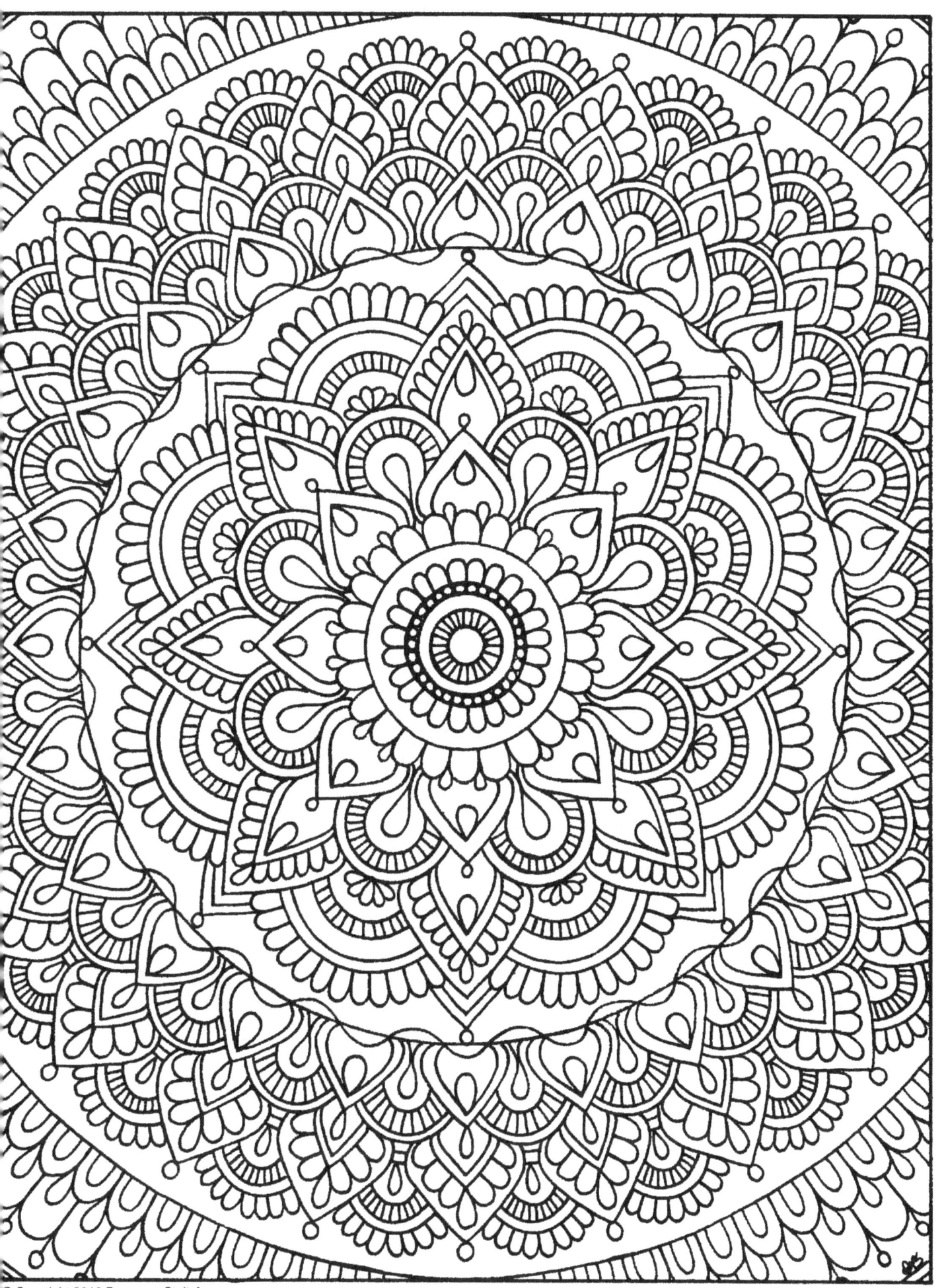

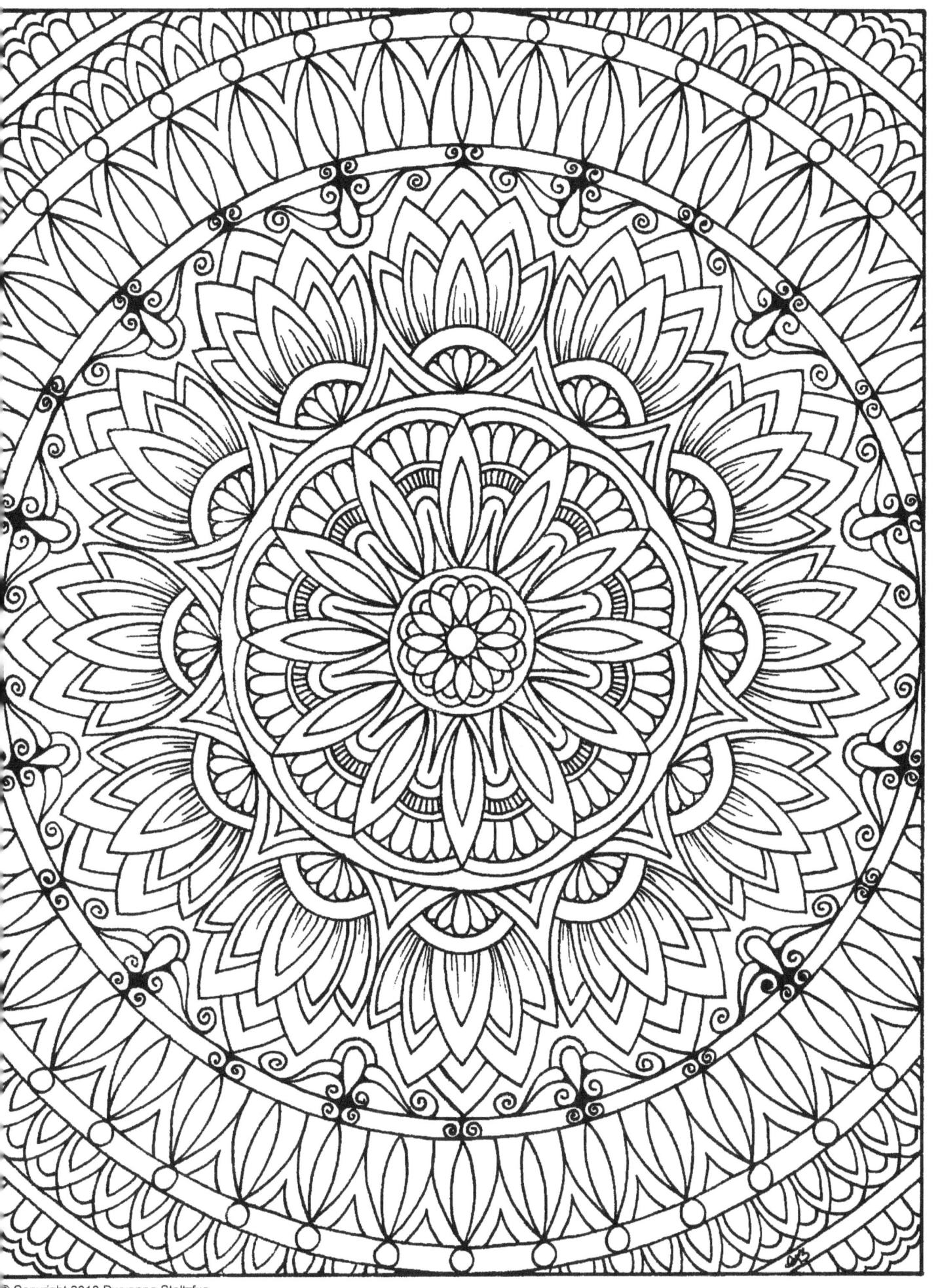

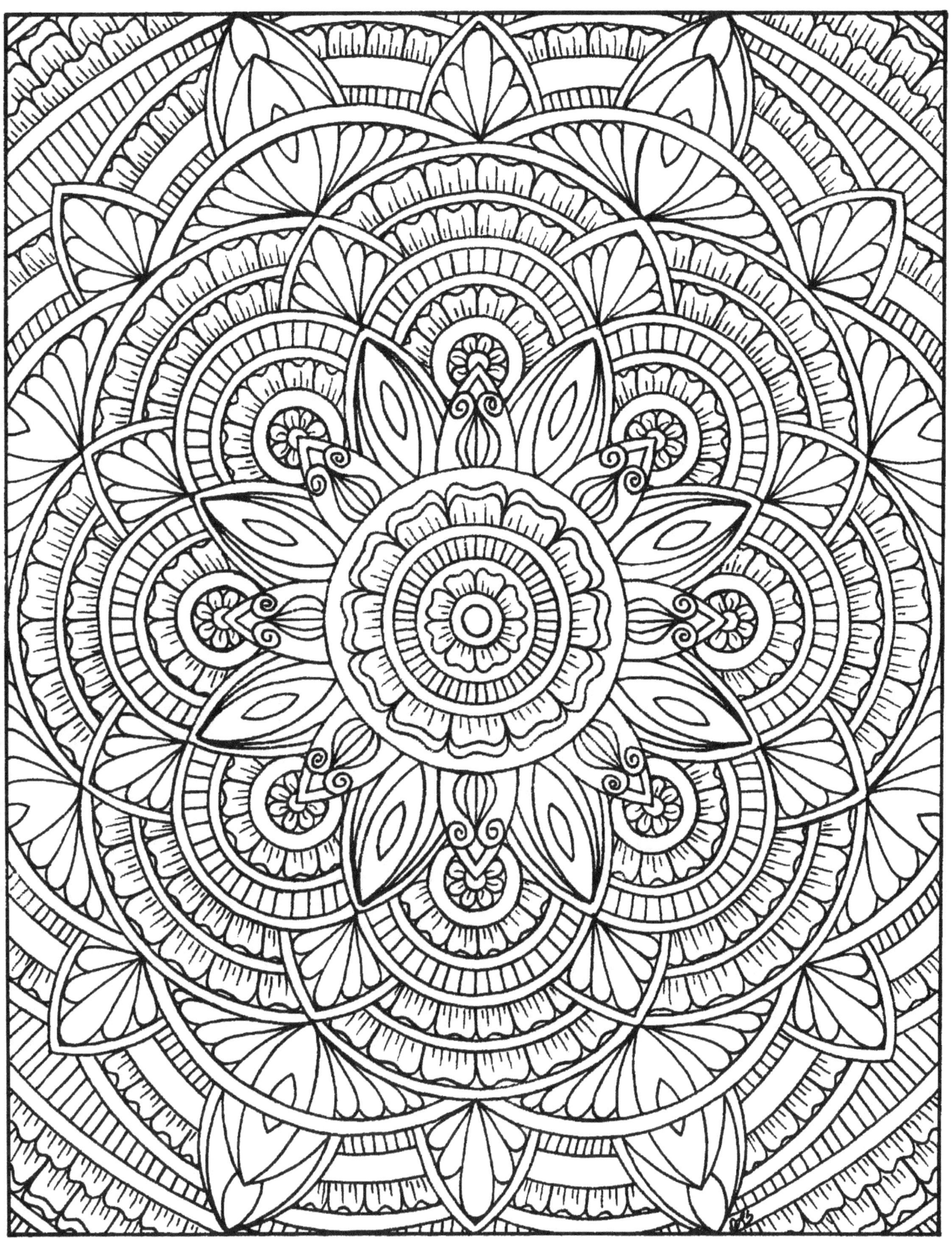